Dionne Vernon,

Thanks for your support. Life is full of wonder — enjoy!

Know yourself
Grow your knowledge
Sow generously to others

That's how you "quilt a life!"

Blessings)
Michelle Clifton-Lucas

Quilting a Life

Piecing together livelihood, lifestyle and life dreams

Michele Claybrook-Lucas
CMC Communications

Copyright © 2003 by Michele Claybrook-Lucas
CMC Communications

All rights reserved. No part of this book shall be reproduced or transmitted in any form or by any means, electronic, mechanical, magnetic, photographic including photocopying, recording or by any information storage and retrieval system, without prior written permission of the publisher. No patent liability is assumed with respect to the use of the information contained herein. Although every precaution has been taken in the preparation of this book, the publisher and author assume no responsibility for errors or omissions. Neither is any liability assumed for damages resulting from the use of the information contained herein.

ISBN 0-7414-1680-8

Published by:

519 West Lancaster Avenue
Haverford, PA 19041-1413
Info@buybooksontheweb.com
www.buybooksontheweb.com
Toll-free (877) BUY BOOK
Local Phone (610) 520-2500
Fax (610) 519-0261

Printed in the United States of America

Printed on Recycled Paper

Published October 2003

Dedication

This book is for my daughter Ciara. I hope that your quilt is colorful, warm and authentic.

To my husband Vernon. Thanks for your support.

Special thanks to:

My mother and father: Mr. Bill and Miss Eva. Thanks for your love, support and prayers.

My brothers: Montague and Jason Claybrook. Thanks for cheering me on.

To my "angels", Ramona Chainey and Beverly L. Williams: You are my sister-friends. This would not have been possible without your help. I sincerely thank you.

"The first step to getting what you want out of life is this: Decide what you want"

\- Ben Steiner

Table of Contents

Introduction i

Part 1: Your Livelihood

1: It's Off to Work We Go!
(Choosing the Fabric for Your Quilt) 1
2: Who Altered the Script?
(Selecting Templates) 12
3: The Malformed Piece: Job Loss
(Fixing the short piece) 27

Part 2: Your Lifestyle

4: Breaking the Synthetic Cycle
(Blocking the Blocks) 43
5: Abundance by Planning & Saving
(Joining the Quilt Blocks) 63
6: Minimizing Stress, Maximizing Health
(Adding Borders) 80

Part 3: Your Life Dreams

7: Creating Your Vision
(Preparing the Top Quilt) 107
8: Minding Your Own Business
(Quilting or Tying the Top) 118
9: Putting it All Together
(Attaching the binding) 133

Introduction

One day I volunteered to teach my daughter's Brownie troop the art of quilt making. It seemed like a fairly simple task; the girls would learn a craft, earn a badge and I could meet my annual requirement as a parent partner.

I've enjoyed quilting for many years. Although a lengthy process, sometimes taking years to complete a single quilt, I consider quilting to be a relaxing hobby. The satisfaction of completing a quilt after months or sometimes years of crafting is always very rewarding.

My fondness for quilting assured me that Troop 324 would learn to love quilting as much as I did.

Good Intentions

There are many design options available for quilts. They can be comprised of a single pattern or can contain multiple patterns, called "samplers." I selected a simple quilt pattern for the girls; "Shoo-Fly." The quilt block contained pieces made of eight triangles and five squares.

The simplicity of the pieces and design made it an ideal pattern to initiate fourteen eight year old girls to quilting.

Our troop meeting started by looking at pictures of quilts in a few of the books that I brought to the session. The girls were fascinated by the patterns and beauty of each quilt. As I passed around three of the quilts that I stitched, the beauty and complexity of the quilts' design piqued the girls' interest in learning more about quilt making.

They were anxious to get their project under way. As I passed around packets of pre-cut fabric that I had painstakingly prepared over the weekend and gave everyone their own copy of the Shoo-Fly pattern, I discovered that only one girl in the troop had experience with sewing or threading a needle.

We spent the next 45 minutes learning the intricacies of needle threading and never progressed to the actual piecing of fabric, which is the foundation of quilting.

After the meeting concluded, the troop leader thanked me profusely for spending time with the girls and teaching them how to quilt.

Reflective Aftermath

As I was driving home, I reflected on the day's activity and thought about how little we had accomplished. To my disappointment, we never got to piece the pattern. I was consoled only by the fact that I had taught the girls something useful - how to thread a needle. At some point in life, a button will come loose and require mending. A simple needle and thread will do the trick!

A few months after my Brownie experience, I abruptly decided to leave my job. Although I had been dissatisfied for a year and a half, it was not the optimum time to sever ties with my employer. The economy was doing poorly; companies were down-sizing and the unemployment rate was high. To make matters worse, I really had not given full consideration to what my next career endeavors would involve. However, the growing sensation that I was not being challenged to think and act creatively hastened the intensity of my feeling that it was time to move on professionally.

After submitting my resignation, I planned to use the time away from the office for serious reflection and evaluation of my skills, life and career. I thought of myself as a "phoenix" preparing for a career rebirth.

During my period of "reinvention", I resumed a quilting project that I had neglected for two years. As I pulled the needle through the cloth of a sampler quilt, I looked at the mixture of color and design and thought about how my career and life were similar to the quilt's pattern variation over the last two decades. The different shapes, colors and patterns reminded me of the numerous roles that defined me and my career-life line.

After spending significant time and energy building my career, I was moving away from the corporate structure, industry and familiarity that had financed my life for two decades. Although I was uncertain regarding my next career move, in my heart I knew that I had no desire to return to a similar environment. I was ready to try something new.

The parallel between the sampler quilt and my life experience illustrated a metaphor: making a quilt is similar to making a life.

I held in my hands a sampler quilt; the patterns varied with each panel's block. The pattern that I had been using in my work life had just changed and I was not sure what the next block would resemble.

Life Circumstances Create Pattern Variations

Comparable to making a quilt, as we go through the various stages of life, sometimes the circumstances that we encounter change the pattern of our daily routine or alter our lives completely. Hence, our lives are not comprised of a singular pattern, but multiple patterns like a sampler quilt. When the pieces that normally fit together don't mesh, it is an indication that the pattern has changed and it is now time to work on a different format.

However, unlike a cloth quilt, the quilt design of our life does not follow a well constructed pattern that allows you to see the image that you hope to create. Design changes occur and we are left to ponder the next steps needed to continue the construction.

A pattern change involving our work lives can involve reducing work hours to accommodate childcare, deciding that your current work no longer provides the energy or stimulation, taking a leave of absence as the result of an untimely death of a loved-one, or being terminated.

Conversely, it could mean reentering the work force after the children have reached school age or an untimely divorce has occurred.

A pattern change in our lifestyle could involve rethinking our relationship with money and the accumulation of material items. Whatever the reason, a shift in the pattern will result in reconsideration of the components of our life quilt and if we are resilient, adjustments will be made accordingly.

Event versus Emotional Change Stimulators

Acknowledging the need to change is the easiest part of the pattern shift as it directly confronts us. This acknowledgment can come in the form of an "event" or an "emotional" indicator that a change is needed.

An event change stimulator comes in the form of an action, such as a lay-off, termination or any life-event that forces a change in the normally established pattern. Event driven change stimulators can be expected or unexpected. In either case, they test our mettle and mental fortitude as the person experiencing this type of change must find reasonable alternatives to adjust to the change. (In quilting, this is analogous to cutting the cloth short and then making alterations to fit the template neatly in the pattern.)

Emotional change stimulators are equally challenging because feelings can generate a persistent longing to try a new career or remake segments of your life. (A new panel design in the "sampler of life.")

My desire to try something new was a result of an emotional change stimulator. Two years prior to resigning from my corporate management position, I informed my husband that I wanted to become a writer.

Emotionally I had made the leap from feeling that I wanted to write something before I die to feeling as though I would die if I did not write. This was a very powerful feeling that affected my career choices when I decided to act upon the emotional change stimulator two years later.

Delayed Response

The suppression of emotions or longings is aided by practical necessity. Sometimes when we vocalize our dreams and inner most desires we are met with disapproving comments or dismissed as unrealistic dreamers. The fear of ridicule or the need to pay bills often supplants the urge to quit the solid nine to five job and "pursue the dream." When this happens we end up living dull lives as monochrome as black and white photographs.

While there are some risk takers, the average person is risk averse when change can be perceived as jeopardizing family finances and personal stability.

I can always spot these colorless lives in an office setting as they routinely go about doing their jobs without interest or zest, secretly or vocalizing their disdain for the job.

Regardless of the stimulator, managing the need to change is often difficult because change upsets the flow of the pattern that has been in effect. It is a rare individual that can boldly embrace a life altering change as a welcomed circumstance whether it is pleasant or unpleasant. Change takes us out of our comfort zone and places us in the dark, scary place called "uncertainty."

Uncertainty creates anxiety and other unpleasant physical effects. It is no wonder that we want to avoid change, even if it means sacrificing personal joy and satisfaction that impacts other aspects of our lives.

Managing uncertainty requires discipline and steely nerves. In order to cope and adjust we must find a way to calm our stomachs, clear our heads and rethink our lives to accommodate change. This process allows us to move forward with our lives.

Something for Everyone

Some people are fortunate to love the professions that they have chosen or have found themselves strategically placed in their current work environment. If you are blessed enough to love your work and have a found the delicate balance between work and life, that's great. This is a reasonable expectation in which we should all strive. Consider yourself fortunate for now.

However, life is not static and you will eventually confront an issue that requires deep reconsideration, re-evaluation or alteration of some aspect of your life. These occurrences are the pieces of life's quilt. This book will provide you with some practical alternatives to consider as well as useful references.

If you are at the same career crossroad where I found myself, then this book may help you address your immediate interest in knowing how to obtain that place of perfect peace and emotional stability where work and life coexist harmoniously.

Considering Life's Components

Addressing career issues is an important component in our life quilt; lifestyle choices and life's dreams are inter-woven in the entire schematic.

This book is about identifying ways to connect our livelihood, lifestyle and life dreams as if we were fashioning a sampler quilt. It's about knowing when and how to shift the pattern to create a different square when event and emotionally driven change stimulators occur instead of experiencing devastation and despair. It's about finding and embracing our true selves and enhancing our character. It's about confronting our fears and finding our joy.

The piecing together of life's circumstance with meaningful work or finding the joy in our current work is essential to creating equilibrium (our livelihood finances our lives!), resulting in a "rich, full and satisfying life." Personal satisfaction is the foundation fabric in life's quilt; spirituality and recognition of a higher power are at the center square.

The events that you confront on a daily basis, the ever-changing circumstances, your physical state and mental well being are all components of the quilt.

The successful merging of these pieces can create a life that you will find enriching and welcoming to everyone whom interacts with you.

About This Book

This book is written from a practitioner's perspective. Using my management and personal experience accumulated over two decades, I provide my viewpoint, experiences and observations regarding the possibilities for finding satisfying work, creating a fulfilling and meaningful lifestyle and making your dreams a reality.

Just as a quilt is made from separate pieces before joined together, this book separates issues which impact livelihood and behaviors that determine your lifestyle before presenting ideas for realizing your life dreams.

This book is a partnership; I present ideas and examples to stimulate your thinking and you use the methods that you feel are most appropriate and adaptable to your life. For example, I resigned from my job, without having another job immediately in sight. However, I know enough about my skills, personal resilience and ability to reinvent myself to understand that this was an acceptable alternative for me.

I had a great passion to pursue a writing career and solid ideas to create a game plan that would bring this dream into fruition. Most importantly, I had savings and family support on which I could rely while I reassessed my life and developed my career strategy.

Would I recommend that you quit your job without having a plan B immediately in sight? Absolutely not! If you have resources to pay your bills and meet your financial responsibilities then it is a reasonable option. However, you should never compound one life-altering situation by adding another to it. It is mentally overwhelming and self-destructive. Use some of the tips in this book to develop a strategy that is reasonable and acceptable based on your self-knowledge.

What This Book Is Not

While this book addresses some lifestyle issues such as body image and eating habits, it does not attempt to delve into topics such as anorexia or bulimia. These are serious eating disorders and there are a variety of books available written by skilled professionals that speak to these conditions.

Any reference to eating in this book involves lifestyle changes that can be made "voluntarily" through behavior modification.

The Book Road Map

"Quilting a Life" is divided into three parts. The first part considers situations that can impact our livelihood; career burn-out, work/life balance issues and job termination. These events serve as sampler designs for our life quilts.

The first three chapters examine the emotional and event change stimulators which serve as indicators that a pattern change is emerging. Resources are presented as a guide to help arrange your life patterns and cope with change. These resources are provided to ignite your curiosity about the possibility that exists for your life.

Just as quilts have an infinite amount of design possibilities, so does your life. While your specific situation may not be covered open your mind to the possibility that some parallels may exist. Use that energy to alter your life's quilt design.

Part two addresses the impact of lifestyle issues. Chapters four through six provide insight into our relationships with material items, perception of wealth, financial capability and self-image. Some ideas for budgeting and saving are provided to help you create your personalized budget. These thoughts can be used to develop a financial plan to fund your life dreams.

Part three examines life dreams and provides suggestions for moving from "day dreaming" to "life scheming." We will examine tools for developing a business plan and learn how to create a strategy to move your dream to reality.

Lastly, all of the names that are used in the anecdotes presented in this book have been changed, to preserve the anonymity of the people who have been referenced.

Let's get started. We're going to separate all the pieces, examine them closely and learn how to thread everything together to create a beautiful, comfortable and colorful life quilt. Everyone's pattern will be different, but they all have the potential to be created masterfully and wonderfully.

I hope that this book will provide you with the insight you need in order to quilt your life.

Part 1: Your Livelihood

The Fabric…
The Templates…
The Patterns…

It's Off to Work We Go!   1

(Choosing the Fabric for Your Quilt)

> *"There is a vast world of work out there in this country, where at least 111 million people are employed in this country alone – many of whom are bored out of their minds. All day long." – Richard Nelson Bolles*

Making a quilt is a lengthy process. Once the quilt pattern has been selected the quilt maker carefully considers fabrics containing colors that will highlight their interpretation of the pattern's design.

The fabric selection is based upon the quilt maker's understanding of the pattern and color preference. Two different individuals could use the same quilt pattern and yield different looking quilts. This is because the quilt maker's preference for texture and color will determine if the fabric will be solid or print, light or dark, primary or pastel colored. These factors will determine the appearance of the finished product.

Grow Up and Get to Work

It seems so simple. If we are fortunate enough to be blessed with good health, then we are conditioned from early childhood that once we become adults, we will work.

Initially, it comes in the form of a simple question that we ask our children, "What do you want to be when you grow up?" Or perhaps it comes through subtle cajoling from family influences to maintain the family business.

Whatever the source, the perception and purpose for work is formed by our caregivers. This is a perfectly reasonable acculturation process since finances are essential to supporting a lifestyle. It is reasonable that parents/caregivers want to raise children who will ultimately contribute economically to society and function independently.

When I was growing up, my father was adamant that I obtain a college education. In his mind, as well as that of a lot of other parents, education was the key to gaining exposure to greater economic opportunity. From a practical perspective, most parents want their children to reach adulthood and find work so they can gain financial independence and cultivate lives of their own. Idealistically, parents want their children to aspire to an economic status which exceeds or at least matches the level that they have attained. Hence, the indoctrination into a work ethic occurs early and is reinforced often in our lives.

The Satisfaction Void

The greatest impact of this early messaging is that it leaves us with the notion that finding work is necessary; finding satisfaction in your work is unimportant. The issue of enjoying the selected livelihood is never a topic of discussion.

My parents were raised during the Depression, a time when work was scarce. Finding employment was viewed as a privilege; the consideration of personal satisfaction with the actual work performed was never an issue. The satisfaction came from being able to provide food and shelter for the family.

These messages were subtly transmitted to the children in our family. No wonder so many of us fight back the aching feeling of discontent. There is no model for "enjoying a job."

Enjoyment is insignificant; the key factor is to generate income. Acknowledgement of these feelings has not been coded into our work ethic matrix.

During the 20 years that I managed and coached people, I often encountered employees who were dissatisfied with their job. Due to the nature of my management rotations, I spent about 6 years managing various service/processing and call center environments. These are the types of jobs that you don't dream about doing when you're growing up.

"Processors" never appear at the school career day. But these are important jobs that must be performed in any organization. These jobs are repetitive in nature, focusing on quality versus creativity.

Although call centers are not processing operations, the job's responsibilities share the same functional repetitiveness. Staff boredom and burnout were frequently observed during my time as a call center manager.

Call centers normally have high employee turn-over rates. The phone center that I managed had a high percentage of recent college graduates hired as phone representatives. On average the phone representatives lasted 18 months before seeking alternate employment due to the repetitive nature of the job. Although staff supervisors initially approached their jobs with enthusiasm, invariably the issue of boredom or feeling a void in their contentment with the job became the focus of coaching sessions around their second year in the assignment.

Regardless of the assignment, as the novelty of the job wore away, boredom and dissatisfaction became an issue for the entire staff. Coaching sessions revealed that individuals were not interested in identifying their true interests but finding the next opportunity that would lead to the next level and higher salary. These objectives perpetuated the cycle of chasing dollars and experiencing monotony.

The Money Trap

Everyone understands that the purpose of work is to earn money. Money pays bills, supports families, funds vacations and purchases food and clothing. However, the necessity of meeting life's financial demands often leaves little time to consider the concept of self-actualization. This is particularly true when we are new to the work force and wanting to start our work lives as encoded during early childhood.

Self-actualization involves defining what is important to you, then engaging in self-development activities that will help you to realize what you've determined to be your life's purpose. Sadly, I had worked for a company for 13 years, abhorring every moment. I stayed there because 1) I was well-paid and the money afforded an enjoyable material lifestyle and 2) I thought that being happy at work and with work was frivolous. For me, happiness was to be reserved for time away from the job when I connected with friends and family. Ironically, I spent long hours at work, leaving me too exhausted to spend time with family and friends during non-work hours.

This is one of the paradoxes of the money trap; working for a lifestyle that is not fully enjoyed due to the emotional drain which results from working a job that is not mentally stimulating or is physically draining. As time elapsed with the organization, my belief that satisfaction and work could coexist moved further from my conscience. I successfully suppressed my emotional change stimulator for over 10 years before taking action.

Recollection of my own experiences caused me to ask the staff supervisors during coaching sessions to focus on the most enjoyable aspects of their jobs and identify the things that they found most stimulating. Their responses included liking their coworkers and other friendly relationships that had been cultivated on the job and within the organization, but did not include the actual responsibilities of their job.

When I asked them to remove the work relationship component and consider the activities they found most stimulating about their job function this seemed to stymie even the most loquacious supervisor. Even after contemplating the question, the answer revolved around some aspect of financial security or benefit and never got to the root of the question.

I realize that working in a repetitive environment does not often generate stimulating and creative thoughts – even if you are the supervisor. In spite of their varied tasks, the supervisors were as bored as their direct reports. Imagine, being involved in a task or function for 8 plus hours daily in which you derive little to no stimulation. The tedium makes for an extremely long day which sucks the energy out of the most enthusiastic person before lunch.

Satisfying Work Supports Satisfying Life

Preferably, the attainment of financial rewards should result in increased personal satisfaction especially if you enjoy the work where you spend the majority of your time. (An average work day ranges between eight and ten hours, more if you bring work home.) The ability to enjoy material excesses increases with the amount of cash that is available to spend. Under these circumstances the worker can sit back and reap the benefits of their labor and experience the internal joy of material satisfaction.

These people are happy and their happiness permeates through every aspect of their lives. Their friends, family and associates benefit from the contentment that they feel. As a result, they are more productive at work and experience fewer sick days.

Each work day is viewed as a new opportunity to write a chapter in their lives. These are the folks who find it incredible that they get paid to do their jobs. Unfortunately, not everyone can boast of this type of work-induced euphoria.

Dissatisfaction Breeds Contempt

If you spend the majority of your day at a job that you dislike, it drains you emotionally, spiritually and physically. Emotionally, you feel trapped by the money that you are making and feel as though you lack options to obtain alternate employment with comparable income potential.

Spiritually, you begin to doubt your purpose in life. Your imagination becomes fertile with self doubt as it seems as though everyone around you is productive and fulfilled except for you. Doubt dominates your thoughts as you begin to believe that there is no other use for your talents or that you even possess talent.

Physically you feel tired. Every morning you pound on the alarm clock snooze button about five times, dreading getting out of bed. Every sniffle or cough results in a "sick day", a chance to get away from work and mentally decompress. Your reality becomes the drudgery of the job that has you financially trapped.

In addition to hating your livelihood, you hate the happy people at work that you believe are not experiencing the same feelings of despair and despondency.

You know that you have reached the bottom when "Thank God it's Friday" and "Living for the weekend." become your personal mantras.

Although these negative, energy draining feelings are common, they do not have to become your reality.

Turn Negativity into Kinetic Energy

Negative self talk only exacerbates your feelings of despondency so if you are transmitting negative internal messages – stop immediately! It's time to focus on healing by creating a plan of action that will energize you. If you are in a job that you find dissatisfying, then it is time to move on. A simple job rotation may give you the boost you need. Before you tender your resignation, identify the source of your discontentment to avoid landing in a similar situation with another department or employer.

With some time and thoughtful preparation, you can find meaningful, satisfying work that will provide financial rewards by taking these steps:

1. **Identify the core of your dissatisfaction:** Are you having problems with your boss or co-workers? Do you dislike the organization's culture? Are you unhappy with your pay? Is the commute too long? Is the work repetitive? Do you feel underutilized? Do you feel over-worked? Every issue that is displeasing to you should be placed on a list. The length of this list will vary for every individual. Try to be constructive as you create this list. Stay away from comments like, "I hate my boss because he has the personality of a stone." That might be true, but at some point in our work lives we all encounter someone who is lacking social and interpersonal skills. This creates an opportunity to demonstrate professional maturity and to learn all you can during time spent with a "social misanthrope" then move on to another assignment. Make this list relevant and real for your personal use. It does not matter if the list has two items or twenty. What matters is that this is the list of issues that are zapping your energy and you need to identify root causes before creating a remedy.

2. **Identify the things that you enjoy about the job:** This is helpful. Since there are no absolutes, although overall you may find the job abhorrent, there may be several enjoyable aspects of the job that you would like to replicate in a new position. Try to focus on the actual tasks that you perform as opposed to the relationships that you've built. We always manage to develop friendly relationships at the work place but you should not focus on those

pleasant interactions during this activity. You want to clearly identify the job activities that you find enjoyable. You'll need to access this list later as you determine your skill set and compare the two lists.

3. **Compare the likes and dislikes:** Put the lists away for a day or two and then revisit them to determine if you have objectively captured your feelings about the job. Compare the lists. If you have several pages of "dislikes" versus "likes" then it is clear that it is time to consider other employment options. However, if your list of "likes" is longer than "dislikes" then perhaps you can increase your satisfaction quotient by changing assignments within the company.

4. **Seek informational interviews:** Contact other departments and request meetings to garner information about their functions in order to determine if your skills would be a good match for another area. Don't be discouraged if you don't get responses to your initial requests for meetings. Find another contact and request another meeting. Become relentless in your pursuit of information. Make this your mission.

5. **Check the posting board:** Sometimes when applying for a job, we forgo true interests for the opportunity to "get a foot in the door." If you have successfully met your residency requirement time in your current assignment, then check out the internal job posting board. Perhaps an assignment that is better aligned with your skills and qualifications is open. If so, then go for it. However, remember that your current department has invested some time in training you, so make sure that you have spent sufficient time in the

department before looking to exit. This is especially important if you want to stay in the organization. It is best avoid creating "hard feelings" that may produce internal road blocks that may surface later in your organizational career.

6. **Seek out mentor relationships:** Traditionally, mentors approach employees that have been identified as having demonstrated advancement potential. However, it is acceptable for you to approach individuals in your organization that you believe can provide helpful career guidance. Ask for coaching. Articulate your interest in obtaining sage advice regarding your career management. Most people are willing to provide assistance. However, if you get a response that indicates the mentor that you selected is not interested – ask someone else. Perhaps their schedule is too full to assume such a responsibility. Don't take it personally. These folks don't know you. Just as you are trying to get your career in order, they are involved in the same process. Keep pressing on until you create a cadre of support to help you navigate your career.

7. **Seek other employment:** Sometimes it is necessary to move away from an employment situation. This option is not for the faint hearted, if it were, more people would vacate jobs due to feelings of dissatisfaction. If you are not sure, then before you move to another job, see number 8.

8. **Take a skills assessment test:** If you are not sure if your current job is a good match for your skills, take a skill assessment to identify your interests. There are some assessments tools available free of charge on the web. Try:

The Birkman Method career interest test:
www.review.com/career/careerquizhome.cfm?menuID=0&careers=6

The Career Key:
www.careerkey.org/english

Motivational Appraisal of Personal Potential:
www.assessment.com

The Explore-Reflect-Act Model:
www.1.umn.edu/ohr/ecep/ERAmodel.htm

Personal Nature and Performance Assessment
www.careerexplorer.net

The Keirsey Temperment Sorter
www.keirsey.com

The Oxford Capacity Analysis Test
www.scientology.org/oca.htm

Mind Frames Personality Assessment
www.initforlife.com

Assorted Personality and Personal Interests
www.2h.com/personality-tests.html

Your Job is Your Life's Fabric

Fabric is the key component to quilt making. It is impossible to create a quilt without fabric. It is the quilt maker's personal preference that will determine the quilt's finished appearance. For this reason, quilt making is a long and contemplative process. Quilt making is not to be approached with the intention of hasty completion. That would result in a sloppy finished product. Quilting is an art form. It is meant to be reflective, relaxing and recreational. The finished product is beautiful and represents the craftsmanship and care that has gone into its construction.

If a protracted period of sedentary handwork is unappealing to you, then you would not be interested in making a quilt.

Life, if you're blessed, will be a long process as well. However, you don't have the option of excusing yourself from working on your life quilt – it's something that's got to be done. You will have the opportunity to select some of the templates that will shape your life; others will be handed to you and you'll simply have to work it out.

If persistent job dissatisfaction plagues you, then perhaps you are not giving sufficient contemplation to the selection of the templates that form your livelihood. Similar to fabric, your job is the essential component to creating your life quilt. A job provides the income you require to cover the basics life needs: food and shelter.

Studies have revealed that on average, a person will have at least five jobs over the course of a lifetime. This means that your first job is probably not your last job. If this is your fifth job and you are still unhappy, then perhaps you have not taken the time to assess your interests. Do it now.

Your work life consumes a lot of time and sets the emotional groundwork for other aspects in your life. Satisfaction with your livelihood is crucial to your overall satisfaction and well-being.

When considering a career or job change it is important to engage in a well thought out plan that will stop the emotional drain and reconnect you with a positive self-affirming mindset. This may seem difficult, but it is possible.

The self-assessment tests will prove to be the lynch pin to connecting your life dreams (or at least to the things you truly enjoy) with your potential livelihood. We will revisit these assessment tests in later chapters, so keep your results close by so that you can refer to them often.

Who Altered the Script? 2

(Selecting Templates)

"Change is the constant, the signal for rebirth, the egg of the phoenix."
Christina Baldwin

Templates are the individual shapes that determine a quilt's design. Separately, the templates resemble simple circles, squares, rectangles and octagons. However, when sewn together they form patterns with varying degrees of intricacy.

A quilt composed of a singular repetitive pattern creates a simple and consistent design. Over time, the quilt maker becomes more adept in their sewing technique by repeating the same process throughout the design. The panels (the blocks or boxes containing the design) contain no surprises. You know from one block to the next the order that you shall place the templates and how the design will look.

A sampler quilt alters the pattern design as each new block is fashioned. Depending on the complexity of the new pattern additional skills may be required to work the new panel design. Each panel presents the quilt maker with the opportunity to make a new motif. This keeps the project interesting by adding variety to the process.

Life Cycles

It never fails. Just when you have reached your comfort zone, something or someone changes a component in your well ordered world. This is part of the cycle of life. You go through various maturation processes; range of experiences broaden, frame of references widen and the circumstances in which you draw upon these resources change.

Change is a reality of life. Although aware of the necessity and inevitability of change, we are often ill-prepared to manage it. A paradigm change in any component of your life will have significant impact on your work life.

When it comes to our work lives, it is easier to contend with a situation in which you feel the need to change because of dissatisfaction with the current work environment or termination from employment. This provides an opportunity to consider alternatives for how you would like to spend eight or ten hours a day and how you would like to receive payment. However, it is extremely challenging to manage external factors that may cause a change in a work situation you find enjoyable.

Imagine this scenario. You enjoy your job. You're in a supportive environment. You're doing well. In addition to "fitting in" within the organization's culture, you have friends; lots of them. Your work and personal life seem intertwined as you move from the office to countless happy hours or "get-togethers" at your coworker's/friend's homes.

Perhaps you've worked at the company for years. You've survived the child rearing years. Now you're enjoying time alone with your spouse having successfully raised the kids to adulthood and out of the house. You cannot imagine that life could be any better! So with all these good vibes going on, why would any sane person change their circumstances?

Sometimes you select the quilt's templates (your circumstances which impact your life such as marriage and birth) and sometimes the quilt's templates are handed to you (i.e. death, divorce and infirmity). Irrespective of the change's origin, you must find a way to cope with the new condition that is now a part of your life's quilt.

Marriage and Childbirth

While our work lives do consume a major portion of our time, people still find time to marry and have children. I once worked in a company where a lot of the employees "hooked up" due to the extended work hours. With little time left to cultivate relationships outside of work, people were drawn to one another due to proximity and formed romantic liaisons. (Fortunately, I was already married and did not find it necessary to participate in this mating ritual.) Irrespective of where you find your mate, marriage can change the delicate balance which exists in your work world.

Marriage and childbirth are life actions in which you willingly participate; you selected this template. Through your own volition you get married. Through your own participation, you have a child. These issues were planned (or maybe unplanned) so as you engage in the process (i.e. planning the wedding and awaiting your child's arrival) you develop the coping mechanisms to deal with the impact that these changes have on your life.

Friends and family will share advice and anecdotes about their experiences in order to give you a sense of what to expect. You take the information and make mental references to draw upon when needed in the future. Although you may experience anxiety, it is manifested in a manageable form that you find palatable. However, friends and family cannot prepare you for how managing parenting and working will impact your life's balance. This is personal and is based solely on your mental motif and definition of stress.

Elder Care

Caring for an elderly parent can cause similar stress to that produced by juggling children and work. In both instances you are concerned about the quality of care that is needed for your loved one. Your anxiety is heightened as you try to squeeze the care of your parent in with the demands of your job and your personal time.

The anxiety of deciding whether to consider an assisted living facility or home based care wears on you mentally as you go through the motions of your work routine. You feel overwhelmed and restless as you attempt to develop resolutions regarding your parent's care and continue to meet the demands of the job.

The job that you once considered delightful is now viewed as an imposition as you struggle to find adequate time to care for your parent and ward off the perception that you are distracted and disconnected from the job.

Work Culture verses Work and Life

Many organizations still function under the premise that employees must separate their work lives from their personal lives. This is really an ironic concept, since your life is a composite of the connection of work and all other activities in which you are involved. The issues that impact your personal life will affect your work life. This is because you can not turn off your brain once you enter the office.

If your organization has a "worker bee" culture, where you are encouraged to work nine, ten, or twelve hours daily, leaving the office after an eight hour stint may cause some raised eye brows. You may even feel guilty that you are leaving after working eight hours and imagine that your peers and management view you as lacking commitment to the job.

As antiquated as the ideal that working long hours translates into heightened productivity these perceptions still exist. I once worked for a company where the CEO distributed a booklet to the employees touting the virtues of working long hours, providing an example which illustrated two employees' workday. Employee A worked a ten hour day, while Employee B worked an eight hour day. The scenario concluded that Employee A would generate 25% more work than Employee B.

In the CEO's illustration, I imagine that Employee A does not have any life issues, since close to 42% of their day is devoted to work. Clearly, Employee A is working with one quilt pattern, they're not working on a sampler quilt – there's no time left in the day!

During my career, I've frequently worked with the Employee A prototype. The CEO's example fails to factor in how Employee A formats their daily agenda in preparation for the planned work day marathon. It generally works like this: Employee A will spend at least 1 hour of the ten hour day taking the standard "joy" breaks.

"Joy" breaks are the little snippets of down time that an employee normally uses to chat with co-workers, visit the snack machine or go the restroom. However, in anticipation of the ten hour day, Employee A will take the standard cumulative sixty minute "joy" break in addition to an extra thirty minutes used to casually inform coworkers and the secretarial staff of their intention to stay late, specifically stating ten hours.

This process generally works best if the manager is within earshot. If the manager has not been presented with the opportunity to learn of the planned ten hour day, then it is standard operating procedure to send an e-mail at an extremely late hour to document that work was being "accomplished" when other mere mortals were sleeping or slacking off with family and friends.

In truth, Employee A spends an inordinate amount of time planning and executing the marketing of the "ten hour day" to the detriment of their effectiveness, which is greatly decreased due to the anxiety created in trying to make everyone aware of their diligence. Moral: Come to the office, do a great job at work, go home at a reasonable hour and enjoy your life.

Change Alters Perspective

When life circumstances require your attention, you must handle then accordingly. Whether your feelings are real or imagined, your quilt pattern has changed and you have to find a coping mechanism. This can be especially challenging if you work in a culture that rewards people who work long hours and do not let personal responsibilities interfere with their work world. Additionally, you may feel stressed as you attempt to keep the same work relationship dynamics in place. Remember the happy hours?

While employed at the "worker bee" organization, I had a discussion with a colleague, Lori, who had recently returned to work after taking maternity leave. Lori revealed that she felt guilty because the 10 hour work day that was previously her typical day was no longer feasible since the birth of her daughter.

Lori's priorities changed and she now preferred to work the standard 8 hours in order to get to daycare before closing and spend time with her daughter before bedtime. This manager's guilt was compounded by the fact that she used to think poorly of women who left the office at the end of eight hours due to childcare. Now she had become one of these people!

Lori was emotionally torn; she had been with the organization for her entire work life and was completely acculturated to the "worker bee" mentality. The change in the dynamics of her personal life conflicted with her work life.

Aside from the cultural conflict, she was satisfied with her job, the organization and the work relationships that she had established during a 15 year period. The adjustments that Lori needed to make were relatively simple. She needed to adjust her personal expectations and let go of the self-imposed guilt.

Although this would have been a relatively simple solution, Lori grew increasingly stressed by her self-imposed pressure to continue to work long hours. The critical comments that Lori had made about others came back to haunt her each day she came to work.

Life Happens

Marriage, childbirth and elder care are not the only life altering events that can impact your work life. A death of a loved one or a divorce or something as mundane as a relocation, which causes your commute to increase, will change the energy that is directed towards work. This does not mean that your level of commitment has decreased; it means that you have another variable to consider.

Although you may have once enjoyed an environment in which work and life merged perfectly into one complete pattern, you must now accept that you are operating under a completely different paradigm.

Accept that Situations Change

The first step to finding a new balance is to accept that situations change. If you are not changing, you are not growing as a person. Whatever life change you are now attempting to address in order to define a new equilibrium, embrace it. If you are newly married, adjust your work schedule to make time to cultivate your relationship with your spouse. Marriage is a significant life change and it must be granted the same careful attention required for a newly planted garden - or else it will be overrun with weeds and die.

Look in the mirror and tell yourself that your spouse is important. Your spouse loves you. Remind yourself that the job has no emotional attachment to you. News flash – you are expendable. If you leave the job today, someone will pick up your work load and the organization will move on as if you never existed. However, if you alienate your spouse due to the extended hours that you spend at work, the damning effects to your relationship may be profound. This may sound harsh but, if you are racked with guilt about tending to personal issues, you need to remind yourself of these facts.

This exercise is equally important when you become a parent or must contend with caring for an ailing loved one or are struggling with your own health issues. Your family and your health should be your first priority. Learn to separate your work life from your personal life, but take care to give the appropriate attention to each component.

Time to Heal

Death is part of the cycle of life. Whether someone that you loved suffered a protracted illness or died suddenly, the impact is the same. You feel pain. It is as if a chunk of your fabric has been yanked out of the quilt and all that is left is a gaping hole with frayed edges. When this happens, initially you think that the hole is irreparable. Look at the edges. They are totally ruined. This is what you are feeling emotionally. You are torn up inside. Your world seems lackluster and pointless. The activities that once brought you joy seem meaningless and obsolete.

If you are energized by your work, you might be inclined to pour yourself into the job quickly so that you won't dwell on your loss. This is a mistake. A loss of a loved one is significant. Take time to heal. Assign the proportionate level of importance to your life and your job. Your job provides the financial means to have a life. Do not become lulled into believing that your presence is essential and irreplaceable on the job. There is someone at the office that can pick up your work load while you are taking time off.

During my corporate career, I had the occasion to observe how colleagues and direct-reports reacted to death and divorce. (The effects of divorce are very similar to death, as it represents the loss of a significant part of your life.) I can recall one chilling incident where one of my staff's daughters drowned in a pool accident.

After three days at home, Delores returned to work because she felt that the distraction of work would help ease the pain of the loss. It did not. A lot of time was spent crying at the desk (understandable) and creating distress for coworkers.

When I asked Delores why she did not take some time off to heal, she replied that she did not want to get further behind in work. Delores did eventually take a leave of absence but whenever I reflect upon her situation I am amazed that in the midst of her intense emotional pain, she chose to value work above her own need to heal.

Committed or Out of Control?

There is nothing wrong with feeling connected or committed to your job. This is the foundation of the work ethic. You spend a lot of time at your job and perhaps you have spent many years building your career through hard work and continuing education. Perhaps it is a source of pride for you and, if so, this is perfectly acceptable. However, remember it is a job, a place of business. Commitments should be reserved for other people, who can reciprocate and hopefully appreciate this type of emotion. A job, no matter how enjoyable, cannot return your deep feelings of devotion and commitment.

Seeking a holistic balance between work and life will be mentally satisfying and enjoyable in the long run. Irrespective of how much you enjoy your job, you must make time to develop other satisfaction outlets. Why? One day you will retire. It is never a good idea to become one dimensional. This limits your conversation and life perspective.

Imagine your "party" conversation if the only topic you feel comfortable discussing is your work. You limit your opportunity to experience life and become an interesting person when you fail to take advantage of the myriad of activities that are available in your community away from your work environment.

Challenge yourself to experience new venues for meeting people who are different than you. A variety of experiences and people creates a lot of possibilities for new adventures. Don't discount the importance of expanding your personal portfolio of friends and acquaintances.

Handling It All

Changing jobs due to difficulty balancing life issues with work is not always the appropriate course of action, especially if you take pleasure in many of the aspects of your work life. Before you hastily submit a resignation, consider the following:

1. **Discuss options with your employer:** Perhaps a recent life event has made continuing your present work load unbearable. If so seek temporary adjustment of your work schedule. Explain your challenges, but also articulate the commitment that you feel towards the job. Create a dialogue that may result in some ideas for balancing life and work. Perhaps your company will consider telecommuting or a part-time schedule that will allow you to find the equilibrium that you need to accommodate life changes. If you are in a profession that allows you to operate independently, such as medicine or law, cut back and rearrange your hours to fit your life's schedule.

2. **Consider a temporary leave:** Time away from your job is essential for emotional healing and your overall well-being. Request a leave of absence. Regroup, renew, re-generate your personal energy. Use the time off to reflect on your situation and connect with your spirituality. During this time you may benefit from seeking guidance from clergy or a

counselor. Perhaps you can draw strength and support from family and friends. Regardless of your preference, use these resources to replenish yourself. The time off will allow you to return to your job invigorated and prepared to connect with work again.

3. **If you are sick, take disability leave:** A legitimate physical ailment is your body's signal informing you that something is not quite right. Instead of going to work, seek medical care and advice regarding your recuperation. If necessary, your doctor may suggest that you take a medical leave. Heed the advice. Most employers offer this benefit, so if you are feeling poorly, take time off to heal yourself. Of course, check first with your Human Resources department to get details regarding this benefit. Next consult with your doctor to ensure that you have a legitimate concern that will qualify for short-term disability benefits. Your employer is not going to appreciate you more if you drag yourself into the office every day. The work will get done in your absence. Your health is your priority, not your employer's.

4. **Redefine your job to accommodate alternative work solutions:** Talk to your employer about non-traditional options such as job-sharing and flex-time. Enter the discussion with a salient plan and suggestions regarding how the idea can work. Focus on the winning results and benefits that your suggestion can generate if implemented. Come prepared to illustrate how you will account for the time spent away from the office. Reinforce that you are serious about your position and that this will allow you to address some life issues that will result in you being refreshed for the job. Stay positive during your presentation. If your manager

asks to think about it, then don't automatically view that as a negative response. He or she may have to sell the idea to a higher level, so be as descriptive as possible in your presentation, including illustrations and examples of how this alternative can work.

5. **Down–size your life:** If you can afford to do so, consider employment that you find equally enjoyable but that requires fewer hours on the job. Working fewer hours may translate into less pay, so you'll need to carefully assess your budget and trim a few expenses in order to make this a stress-free alternative. If you have a financial partner or spouse, get them involved in the process. There's nothing worse than having a great idea without your significant other's support. Remember, a life down-sizing impacts everyone in the house. Both you and your partner will have to create lists identifying things that you both can live without. Prepare yourself. This is not an easy discussion. Folks get very territorial when it comes to asking them to give up stuff that they enjoy, so expect to have multiple discussions around this subject. Try to concentrate on the long term effects that down-sizing will have on your life instead of the immediate impact of sacrificing the "extras." Remember the reason for considering this option. Long-term, this will provide you with the mental stimulation that you need in your work life while allowing you the time to sort through personal issues at home.

6. **Start a home based distributorship:** Consider employment opportunities that can be done from inside your home. If you can find the space and the time to work within your home, free from the distraction of children and household

responsibilities, consider this as an option. There is plenty of home based business information on the internet. Surf the web and research those businesses that appeal to you. These companies generally require a nominal start-up fee which will cover the cost of the product and market material provided. The amount of creating and development is minimal since you are serving as a franchisee for someone else's business. However, if you lack discipline, focus, personal drive and motivation or need the companionship of office mates, this may not be a viable solution.

7. **Start your own business:** Do you have a marketable skill that will allow you to generate income? If you have the ability to create a workable, relevant business plan and the wherewithal to execute the plan through a well-thought strategy, then give it a try. However, the same rules apply as in number 6, if you lack drive, motivation and focus or lack the capital to maintain your life while you are getting established, this might not be the option for you. If you have a strong desire to become your own boss and you are determined to give this a try then investigate some other businesses that operate in the same market you are considering. We'll discuss this option in detail in Chapter 8.

8. **Stay at home and reevaluate your priorities:** If you have sufficient savings or your spouse's income can carry the financial load and your spouse agrees to this, then go for it! This option can provide the opportunity for deep reflection of your life. In the quiet of your home, think about where your have been in your career. Where you would like to go in the future? How you can manage your new life circumstance with the career? Perhaps a

job change is the answer. Maybe you will change careers. Who knows? Only you can figure this out by carefully evaluating the priorities in your life and determining which course of action you should take.

9. **Check out the web for additional resources:** Still not sure if you need to make some changes? Try the following websites to get some confirmation of what you may be feeling:

Work Life Balance Quiz:
www.quintcareers.com/work-life_balancequiz.html
www.lifelearninginstitute.com/cgi/lliquiz.pl

Stress Management Assessment:
www.stressdiagnosis.com
http://stress.about.com

Elder Care:
www.careguide.com/careguide/index.jsp
www.elderlawanswers.com
www.elderweb.com
www.asktransitions.com

Home-Based Telecommuting Opportunities:
(Telecommuting friendly companies and job listings)
www.work-at-home-dot.com
www.wahm.com
www.2work-at-home.com
www.workathomecentral.com
www.ivillage.com

Home-Based Distributorships
www.paycheckforlife.com
www.coastalvacationswholesaleclub.com
www.homebusinessmatchmaker.org

Life Circumstances are Your Quilt's Templates

Pattern changes that alter life situations are not as welcomed in life. The process that makes quilting interesting, adding various layers of complexity and multiplicity, creates stress when it occurs in life.

When making a fabric quilt, the artist has the option of selecting the pattern that will form the design. However, the templates that form your life quilt are sometimes selected for you. When these templates are placed squarely in your hand, you have no recourse but to pick them up and use them in your quilt. Unfortunately, you don't always know what the design will resemble with these new and unexpected "pieces." You must develop a certain resilience in order to acknowledge, assess and then act upon the changed circumstances.

The need to juggle and reconfigure routine due to a change in life style is common. Remember, whatever situation you are experiencing, chances are that you are not a trailblazer. With that in mind, develop a network of resources to obtain information and ideas regarding how you can manage your situation.

Start with resources that provide you with the most comfort. This could be family and friends, or your church or other community resources. Perhaps you need to start with quiet meditation to clear your head and connect spiritually regarding the issues that you are confronting.

The objective is not to hand your concerns to other people for resolution. Rather, your goal is to garner information and spiritual and emotional strength, so that you can develop some alternatives for managing your life. In the process you may even gather some leads regarding other "family friendly" employers that may be better suited to you if your current employer is unreceptive to the ideas suggested above.

Perhaps you can become part of a support group which focuses on your particular issue. Remember there are resources available. Use them.

The Malformed Piece: Job Loss   3

(Fixing the short piece)

> *"Getting fired is nature's way to telling you that you had the wrong job in the first place."* - Hal Lancaster

The cloth is transformed by the precision in which the quilt maker uses the template and scissors. These individual shapes when sewn together bring to life the pattern's design. It is imperative that the pieces fit together flawlessly. Once assembled these pieces should form a series of perfectly shaped eight inch by eight inch squares. This is the standard dimension for a quilt block. These blocks will be sewn together to form a larger cloth diameter.

Quilting is simply the process of attachment – smaller pieces form bigger pieces that create bigger pieces that eventually develop into the quilt's top. This is called "piecing."

Cloth that is hastily cut will produce pieces that are malformed and do not fit together. Fortunately, quilting uses cloth. When you mess up, you cut another piece using the correct sizing in order to fix your mistake.

Life Interrupted

It seems as though it is the most devastating event. You have lost your job. Whether your employer called it a termination, down-sizing, reorganization or lay-off, the end result is the same; you are currently unemployed. Upon close examination, you may be responsible for your own state of newfound leisure, especially if you were terminated due to poor work performance. Perhaps some of the issues discussed in chapter one surfaced before you could manage to deal with your emotional change stimulator.

Maybe your company has reorganized through a merger or acquisition and your job was eliminated. Whatever the reason, your livelihood has ceased generating income at this particular point and you need to quickly determine how to fit this piece of fabric, which has been cut short, into the quilt.

Pink is the Color of a Down-sizing

Well, let's look for the good news. If you were down-sized, perhaps you received a cash payment that will help you pay your bills while you look for other employment. Hopefully, you have a cash nest-egg stowed away for unexpected occasions such as this or maybe you are eligible to receive unemployment. If this is your story then you can take a deep breath and begin to think about what you want to do next with your work life.

A down-sizing can be a time of reevaluation and reflection, especially if you don't have to worry about cash. Did you enjoy the industry in which you just left? Are you in an industry that will continue to experience lay-offs? Did you enjoy this type of work so much that you are willing to risk future lay-offs in this industry? Close examination of these questions can provide you with some ideas regarding your next actionable steps.

If you are in an industry that is experiencing frequent lay-offs, irrespective of how much you may enjoy this type of work, it is an indication that you must gain additional marketable skills that will supplement your livelihood during periods of unemployment. This does not mean that you have to commit to enrolling in a college program. School is not for everyone. However, a dislike for school does not mean that you should not make a commitment to lifetime learning. Check out a certificate program or class at your local adult education facility. A classroom setting is a great opportunity to learn a new skill, meet new people, network and have fun.

You're Terminated

If you gave your best effort, yet got terminated due to poor work performance it is an indication that your skills were mismatched with the job requirements. If it is your honest assessment that you gave the utmost energy and enthusiasm to the job but your performance was not in sync with the responsibilities or the objectives of the job, then it is time to reconsider alternatives. You will continue to experience diminishing returns if you pursue employment for which you are ill-equipped no matter how much energy you expend. If you really have passion for the work then use your time off to review the reasons for the termination and acquire additional skills that will better prepare you for future opportunities.

Your entire work history is your personal career inventory or career investment. If the "investments" in your portfolio are under-performing, then it is time to take corrective action. If you have a disdain for formal training, you may have to give this some consideration in order to fortify your skill set. If a classroom setting is unappealing, then seek to gain "hands-on" experience by volunteering in an activity that might support your skill set. Ask your family and friends for suggestions. You will be surprised at the different options that will arise from tapping into other perspectives.

Conversely, if you have been terminated for poor work performance because you intentionally did not do your best work, or for any other reason, it was an indication that it was time to move on. Your indirect response to your emotional change stimulator was to disengage from the job and it resulted in termination. You are now free to pursue other opportunities that may prove more satisfactory.

As a manager, I have had to terminate employees for a variety of reasons, sometimes for work performance but frequently for poor attendance. I can recall one employee that I worked with years ago who was being counseled for poor attendance. Vance appeared receptive each time we spoke and vowed to make improvements. Unfortunately, Vance did not alter his behavior pattern, continued to call out sick and eventually was terminated from the job.

During the termination meeting, Vance sat across from my desk impassively, as if in a semi-hypnotic trance. It was as if he was relieved that he no longer had to show up for a job from which he had long since disconnected. In a case such as Vance, a termination can be viewed as a welcome relief.

So you may be thinking, it is easier to under-perform and warrant termination than to resign from the job – at least I'll get unemployment compensation. Be careful. This is not necessarily true. If you are terminated due to poor work performance your ex-employer has the right to deny any claims for unemployment. Hence, you've compounded your problem by creating a cash shortfall, if you were planning to use unemployment payments to stay financially afloat.

Additionally, your work reputation is damaged if someone in your network remembers your poor performance or directs you to someone who heard of your work issues. It is better to maintain control of your work life than to relinquish decisions regarding your livelihood to others.

A job loss due to poor attendance means that you did not enjoy the job enough to get up and go with any regularity. It also means that you lacked the emotional resources to seek alternatives before losing your job. Only you can identify the reason behind you losing your motivation. It is important to do so before moving to your next job or else you will repeat the same behavior pattern.

We've already identified the difficulty in taking full control of a decision to leave a job, without knowing or understanding where the next employment opportunity lies. This is about control. You are holding the needle that is creating your life quilt. Anytime you relinquish responsibility for your actions, you relinquish a portion of control of your life.

In Vance's situation, he was in a job that provided little stimulation resulting in dissatisfaction. Instead of creating an action plan to move along, he chose to passively sit back and let an action "happen to" him. This type of behavior does not allow for the proper planning needed to rebound and create viable alternatives.

Altered Personal Focus

Just as organizations change their focus and direction when new leadership gains control, your personal focus changes as you grow emotionally and intellectually. This may have been a key contributor to the loss of energy that you chose to expend on the job.

Your job may have become less interesting if you felt as though your values conflicted with the organization's values. You may have gained new skills and felt underutilized in your assignment. You may have perceived that there was no opportunity to use these newly acquired skills or advance any further within the organization. Perhaps after observing the promotional patterns in the organization, you came to believe that you hit the "glass ceiling." Whatever the reason take time to assess while you are away from the job. Now is the time to reflect, review and renew.

Reflect

This is a great time to do some "soul searching." You no longer have to go into the office and mentally multi-task about what you want to do with your life. In the quietness of your home or wherever you find solace, consider what is important in your life and think about the opportunities that you may want to explore.

This is an activity. Get some paper. Write down what makes you happy. Is it money? Is it prestige? Is it time with family and friends? Do you have a strong desire to work for the improvement of your community? Do you like to teach or talk or write? Get it down on paper. This is the impetus for your next career move. What you write on the paper can become an opportunity to create a work life that merges the things that you identify as enjoyable, meaningful and fulfilling.

If you were terminated, something made you disengage emotionally from your previous employer. As you create this list, identify gaps that existed in your prior job and ways to fill those gaps in your next one.

Review

After you've created your personal fulfillment list, it's time to develop the connection to tangible skills. Do some research and gather information regarding careers that might satisfy your personal interests. Utilize personal resources such as friends and family. Visit the library. Use the internet to visit career sites that you have an interest in exploring. Look in the phone book. The key is to identify alternate careers that meet your criteria for fulfillment and income potential. This is not an easy process. It will require diligence, focus and constant involvement of others.

If you are without an income stream during this time, consider part-time employment in order to pay bills. Stay focused. Remember that the part-time job you are working does not represent your life goals. It is a means to getting where you want to go.

Be realistic. Sometimes your need to generate income, especially if you have family responsibilities will defer your plans to leisurely spend time engaged in a protracted period of reinvention and thoughtful meditation. If this is the case, consider getting a job that will meet your financial obligations but continue to explore your interests on a part-time or voluntary basis. Don't rule out volunteering your time. It could lead to a pay for performance opportunity.

In order to pursue my writing goals, I contacted a non-profit magazine and offered to create a monthly column devoted to topics regarding career management. I made my "pitch" more attractive by offering to write the column for free. After submitting two articles and several ideas, the editor decided to pay for my writing services in order to retain me on the staff. Don't be afraid to create the momentum to move your dreams along!

Renew

Surprisingly, after you have expended energy into honestly assessing what your next career moves will be, you will feel renewed! At this point you will have a plan of action in hand and you are prepared for execution. The energy that you feel will spirit you on to the physical task of networking.

Networking

When you are unemployed, it should not be a secret, especially if you are hoping to secure another job. Everyone that you meet or who knows you must be made aware that you "are currently between employment opportunities."

There is no shame in unemployment. It happens. If you got a pink slip and lost your job, you are one of the millions of Americans who have experienced a similar situation. Do not internalize your lay-off with negative self-talk and self-blame. You need a positive outlook and demeanor when you introduce yourself to people.

Networking is not difficult. Imagine throwing a pebble into a pond. The water forms a circle that starts small and increases in width as the circle becomes larger and larger. That's the basic concept behind networking. At the center of the circle are the people who know you best and have a sense of who you are; your family and friends.

Initiate your process of putting the network into motion by informing those closest to you about your employment situation. However, you must provide information, not merely state that you have lost your job. Articulate information about what career or job opportunities you are hoping to pursue. Additionally, you should be able to discuss your skill set and the value that it provides. If you are considering a career change, draw parallels regarding the applicability of your skills in this new career. Boldly market what you believe are your competencies in this new field of interest.

Flexibility is the key when you discuss your career goals because someone may provide a lead that does not "match" your job objective, but may develop into another opportunity. The goal is to get as many contacts as possible. Contacts should not be confused with potential "jobs." Your initial goal is to have as many discussions as possible with folks in your ever-widening circle. You are on a mission to gather information.

The next diameter in your network is your community. Approach your pastor or members of any clubs which you belong and talk about your employment situation. If you are not in any clubs or do not have any community affiliation because you spent long hours on your job and lacked the time to cultivate these types of relationships, this is a great time to get involved. This is also a warning that your life balance may be off kilter if you find that you have little to no resources outside of your former employer.

View this as a timely opportunity to identify activities that interest you and begin to reach out to others. Ask neighbors if they are involved in any community groups. Attend a meeting to see if you are interested in their mission and have something to contribute. Contact your alumni association to learn about social activities that you can attend and reconnect with folks.

If you live near a YMCA, join one of their many volunteer committees. The YMCA usually offers a variety of adult programs that are free or nominally priced.

Emotionally, you will feel better; you become more involved with others and your social circle broadens. Soon you will connect with people that you never knew before. Your possibilities for employment increase with each conversation.

Victor or Victim?

While unemployment due to termination can be a devastating time, it is important to remember that you will work again. Ideally, your next job will be as fulfilling as or perhaps more fulfilling than your previous job. However, you must take an active part in achieving this goal. Let's recapitulate the steps needed to start charting your life plan:

1. **Reflect, Review and Renew:** Although painful, think about the reasons for your termination. Consider acquiring additional skills through classes, internet study and certificate programs. If you intentionally disengaged from your employment situation, identify the reasons. Make a list of things that you value and that provide emotional satisfaction. Connect your "value list" to possible career alternatives. Cross reference your "value list" with your skills assessment list.

2. **Build a Network:** Start with a list of ten people. Call or visit these folks and explain your current employment situation; articulate your career vision and objective (established in #1). Don't leave the conversation without another contact. You want your network to ripple and grow. Remember, as you speak with each new contact, your goal is not to get a job, but to harvest information.

3. **Market Yourself:** You can create a one page website marketing your skills for **F-R-E-E.** There are sites listed at the end of the chapter that provide this

service. Web page creation is made very simple by providing step by step instructions. Make it fun and unusual, but be clear about your career objectives and the skills that you are "selling." As you meet new people, direct them to your website during your conversation. Have some inexpensive business cards made that list your web address and phone number where you can be reached. Every new contact should receive your business card. Make each contact memorable, so that your card recipient will feel motivated to pass your information to other contacts long after your meeting has concluded. Using a website to market your skills sends the message that you are confident and secure in your capabilities. These are qualities that employers are always seeking in potential job candidates.

4. **Stay Active:** You're going through one of the most emotional periods of your work life. You feel bad and your self-esteem is in jeopardy, or perhaps it's already hit the lowest emotional ebb. Get active. If you belong to a gym and haven't gone in some time, dust off the card and get going. You need to be in good physical condition to network and research. This is not the time to compound your situation by becoming ill due to inactivity or gaining weight that keeps you from fitting into your clothes. You will need these outfits for interviews and contact meetings. If you don't belong to a gym, go for a walk. The fresh air and sun will replenish your spirit.

5. **Stimulate Your Mind:** Although you're in a reflective mood, you don't want to spend all of your time cloistered away in meditation. Visit your local library. You'd be surprised at the number of social and cultural activities that are available. The libraries don't require membership in order to attend book readings or financial discussions, however the

membership is *free*, so join! Perhaps you can get involved in one of the many book clubs that are available. Here's another opportunity to connect with other folks, meet new people and expand your growing network. Don't forget to check out your Sunday paper to get information about book readings and signings at local book stores. It's another *free* activity available to get you out the house and involved with other people.

6. **Stay Spiritually Connected:** Things could be worst. You could have a serious illness or become injured in an accident. You lost your job, but you will work again. Remind yourself of this simple fact. Begin each day with the acknowledgement and gratitude that you are healthy, safe and mentally sound. Start your day with a positive affirmation, prayer or meditation. Find a positive quote or bible verse that you find especially uplifting to recite while looking in the mirror each morning. It's not hard to do. As you are putting the toothpaste on your toothbrush, recite your mantra. Believe in the words that are coming out of your mouth. Like yourself. Believe in yourself. If you can't convince yourself of your own value – how can you convince others? This should be a daily task. Use each morning as a time to mentally fortify your spirit by focusing on the good things that are happening in your life. Write them down and refer to them often or when you are combating negative energy. Focus on exuding positive energy and you will receive positive energy in return.

7. **Avoid "Toxic" People:** Perhaps you know other people that have been terminated, downsized or unemployed for a protracted time period and they are miserable. Instead of concentrating on creating positive energy, their philosophy is "Misery loves company." These are the folks who see the glass as

half empty, never half full. They have lost hope and sight of the potential that lies in this challenging moment in their lives. Worst yet, they take comfort in rehashing the past instead of focusing on the future. You need to stay away from these people. You already feel bad. Why exacerbate the situation by sitting around the house all day eating corn chips and complaining or talking about the stupidity of your ex-boss? Keep it real – you got fired. Your ex-boss is still employed. This is counterproductive activity and will not help you with your situation. In fact, it is a waste of time. If you feel the need to be with other people that can empathize with your circumstances, join a support group. The purpose of these sessions is to lift your spirits and provide encouragement. If you must dwell on your past employment situation, beyond the reflection stage, then a positive support group is the only option that you should consider.

8. **Visit the internet to research careers and job sites:** There are a variety of websites that provide advice and information regarding conducting a job search as well as job banks. You can also locate part-time employment as a way to generate income through interim employment. Here are a few sites to get you started:

Job Search Advice, Support Group Chat and Helpful Hints:
www.jobhuntersbible.com
www.jobskills.info

Career Journal in the Wall Street Journal:
www.careerjournal.com

America's Job Bank:
www.ajb.org

Job Seeker Sites:
www.careerbuilder.com
www.bestjobsusa.com
www.careerpath.com
www.careerweb.com
www.americanjobs.com
www.topjobsusa.com

For Diversity Job Seekers:
www.imdiversity.com
www.bestdiversityemployers.com
www.black-collegian.careercast.com

Nation Job Network:
www.nationjob.com

Create our own Website for free:
www.angelfire.lycos.com
www.geocities.yahoo.com

(AOL subscribers)
http://hometown.aol.com/hmtwn.aol.com

Making the Short Piece Fit

During the piecing phase of quilt making, mistakes are often made when cutting the fabric templates. What results is a piece that is ill-shaped or too short to fit neatly into the pattern. A quilt maker always begins a project with the anticipation that mistakes will be made. Hence, there is always extra fabric available to cut pieces again.

Your life quilt has pieces that form your livelihood. Sometimes these pieces are "cut short" causing an interruption in the overall flow of your work life. Although the remedy to reconnecting is not as simple as "cutting a new piece," rebounding is possible by well executed techniques.

Termination from a job is like a piece of fabric that has been cut too short. A job loss breaks the continuity of the life quilt. However, there is rarely an exit plan in place when down-sizing or job loss occurs hence, the replacement of the work "fabric" can be a lengthy process.

As "messed up" as your job loss may seem, you must find a way to work the shortened fabric back in your life quilt. A job termination will alter the pattern, but it does not stop other patterns from taking form. Learn to think creatively about all that you are capable of achieving.

It may be difficult for you to believe or accept this fact; you are capable of doing many things. Consider your job loss as an opportunity to find other employment that is better suited to your skills and interests.

Imagine that you are in a fabric store, surrounded by reams and reams of cloth: cotton, muslin, satin, wool, colors and prints abound! Walk through the aisles, look at the variety and imagine the possibilities. This is your opportunity! You are positioning yourself to create a new design. Make your selection and continue to make your quilt!

Part 2: Your Lifestyle

Blocking…
Joining…
Adding…

Breaking the Synthetic Cycle   4

(Blocking the Blocks)

> *"I'm living so far beyond my income that we may almost be said to be living apart." - e.e. cummings*

One of the first lessons taught in quilting is that an authentic quilt is made from 100% cotton. Pure cotton is durable. The pieces can endure multiple handling without experiencing excessive fraying. Pure cotton quilts can tolerate pulls and cuts and still maintain their beauty and purpose.

As the individual pieces of cloth are assembled and joined to form blocks sometimes the connected blocks form a square that is not symmetrically boxed. If the block is made of pure cotton, then a simple trim around the edges can straighten any asymmetrically shaped block.

Although the blocks made of synthetic fabric have the outward appearance of being durable, the cloth can not withstand multiple handling as it will quickly unravel.

Obnoxious or Obsession

We all like nice things. For me, it's shoes. My love of shoes stems from my childhood. When I was growing up, each year my parents would buy one pair of shoes for me to wear with every outfit.

I remember one particularly hideous pair of olive green oxfords that compelled me to inform my mother that when I became an adult I would own a room full of shoes. True to my word, I have a walk-in closet stacked from floor to ceiling (all four walls) with shoes.

The shoe obsession began in my twenties during the early part of my work life. It seemed as though I worked to buy shoes every pay day. Excited to have an income, I quickly developed an appetite for making shoe purchases that created an image of my "social self" as a shoe savant; an all knowing diva skilled in every aspect of shoe styles, designs and colors. This was my self appointed claim to fame (Hey, I was 22 years old.).

Living the Glamorous Life

Working to buy clothes or other accoutrements that create our physical packaging is done for reasons other than fashion addiction. Everyone has some level of vanity which causes us to want to look a certain way. Our physical presentation, our personal "show", makes a statement about the perception that we want others to publicly receive.

People are visual. Without having the opportunity to know someone personally, we rely on what is visually presented. As a result, your public presentation visually creates your personal statement; your business card to the world. This is a form of self-marketing.

Depending on the objective, the person doing the marketing will transmit their public message through obvious visual effects such as their hair style, clothes, jewelry and car. These are all methods for providing an abbreviated impression regarding our socioeconomic status or the impression we want others to have regarding our socioeconomic staus. Only the individual truly knows and understands the motives behind their social presentation.

I've chosen the following soap opera titles to "broadly" illustrate three types of marketing messages that individuals can send:

1. The Bold and Beautiful
2. The Young and Restless
3. One Life to Live (preferably someone else's life)

The Bold and Beautiful

People in this classification are sending the message that they are financially sound and enjoying the material benefits of their success. Happily, they can afford beautiful clothes, large homes, luxury cars and fantastic vacations. The purchases that are made do not create financial stress – quite the opposite – their purchases bring satisfaction because their sources for income support their chosen lifestyle.

Financially they've checked the boxes on all the essential categories; they are home owners, have funded their retirements and if they have children, have made provisions for college. The disposable income that they spend is their way of saying "I work hard and I deserve to spend my money as I see fit."

If you fit this classification, kudos, you may move on to the next chapter.

The Young and Restless

Unlike the name suggests, people who fall in this classification are not necessarily "young." This persona has no age limit. The Young and Restless (TYAR) create their marketing strategy based on their desire for immediate material consumption. Their income potentially could support their voracious appetite for spending but it's difficult to tell because, irrespective of their income level, they find it necessary to enhance their spending with credit card use (more on this in Chapter 5).

They are willing to make short-term financial sacrifices in order to have the shoes or suit or expensive car today. The sacrifices made are evidenced by the absence of savings or property ownership. TYAR are inclined to spend all of their money on purchases that enhance their appearance. There is a tendency to live with parents or a room mate since their spending habits frequently lead to excessive material consumption, leaving little to no funds for maintenance of a residence.

Living at home with mother does not disturb this personality type because TYAR views this as a conduit to purchasing all of the material goods that they desire, without having to worry about keeping a roof over their heads. Their appearance will market, "Look at me. I look good. I have lots of stuff." Their marketing message is superficial because they own nothing beyond their clothes and car.

In spite of TYAR's tendency to live for the moment, their existence, in the short-run is virtually stress-free. As long as they have money to spend or access to credit, they are satisfied. However, in the long run their stress level will escalate as their spending rate accelerates; resulting in accumulated debt and a low credit rating.

One Life to Live

This individual's marketing strategy is to give the impression of financial well-being, knowing that their income can not support the imagery that they are projecting. One Life To Live (OLTL) believes that everyone is in a better financial position than they. The people used as the standard to be measured against are peers or anyone that has been identified as having the type of lifestyle that they admire and secretly covet (usually The Bold and Beautiful).

Not to be out done, this person will spend their pay and use credit cards to create a façade of well-being and prosperity in order to feel on par with others. Compounding this already stressful endeavor, OLTL will seek opportunities to be in the presence of the people whose lifestyles they seek to emulate.

The OLTL feel compelled to measure up to peers whom they have placed on an imaginary pedestal. OLTLs are the masters of multi-tasking; they can simultaneously admire others while berating themselves for not measuring up financially. They expend their energy cultivating a pretense in lieu of making the changes in their lives that could possibly alter their financial situation. Consequently, the OLTL live a stress filled existence caught between the realization that they live a manufactured life and clueless about how to make constructive changes.

The OLTL's public statement is "I belong, really, I belong."

The Usefulness of Marketing

Most working adults want their public statement to say, "I'm doing well." This is a justification for going to work every day – you have achieved financial stability or you are at least moving in the direction of this goal. If things are going really well, then perhaps you have achieved financial success.

The definition of success, like "self- marketing" imagery, is completely personal. Success could be defined as having completed four long years of college and landing a job, being promoted to a high level post after investing many years with a company, becoming engaged or having a child.

Whatever the definition, it is not merely enough to be satisfied with the personal knowledge that you have achieved these accomplishments. This act alone seems to marginalize the accomplishment. Other people must know what has been achieved; that adds to the joy and satisfaction that you already experience. For some folks, satisfaction can only be attained if others know that you are starring in your own financial success story.

What better way to effectively market an accomplishment or create the façade of achievement (more regarding this later), than to present the outward appearance of having it all together?

The most extreme cases start with the clothes; stylish and possibly fashioned by the trendiest designers, preferably Italian. Nothing subtle here; everyone must know that you are wearing Prada, Gucci and Fendi. The styles selected blatantly scream the designer's name as if you were a human billboard. After describing your outfit from head to toe (and you will describe your outfit), you have spoken a complete sentence in Italian. In your most delusional state you begin to think that you are bilingual.

In order to complement the stylish clothes, the appropriate car must be driven, but not just any car. No Saturn or any other economical, gas efficient model is for you. No way. That would be construed as cheap and cheesy and would never coordinate with the clothes that you've selected. You need something sporty, trendy and eye-catching. Your car must do more than take you from point A to point B; you must turn heads in the process or at least be the topic of conversation once you get to your destination. This is your statement to the world and you are determined to make the most of it.

The above description reflects an extreme situation. Not everyone who wears expensive clothes and jewelry and drives luxury cars is motivated by a desire for the adoration of others. Irrespective of the consumer's motives, these goods are marketed as "status" symbols which make their attainment exclusive and special.

The purchase of a BMW over a Saturn is definitely based on personal preference. However, the marketing that goes into ensuring that the BMW is viewed as a plush, stimulating, pseudo-aphrodisiac car riding experience helps consumers interested in conveying this imagery of exceptionality. The pricing of the car also assures the exclusivity of the vehicle. Not everyone can afford to buy or lease a BMW.

Keeping It Real

There is no shame in wanting to make your presence known; this is how we distinguish ourselves from one another. You want to display your individual uniqueness; it's a way of garnering attention. Mentally, you want to convey the message that you're clever, you're above average, you're not the ordinary person – you're amazing. The clothes, shoes, jewelry and the car you drive reinforce this message to everyone that you encounter.

If you can afford the finest clothes, cars and jewelry and these purchases give you pleasure, then do so. Your consumption of expensive goods is supported by the income that you earn and you are entitled to do as you wish with your finances. The money that you have access to supports this type of lifestyle in a stress free manner. The economy depends on you, so please consume.

However, if you engage in this type of behavior but you frequently find that you have insufficient funds to support this life imagery, then you need to deeply reflect upon your motives for creating this type of image.

Think about this for a minute. If you've developed the habit of purchasing fine things but your cash flow can not support this image that you've created, ask yourself, "Why am I doing this?" If your initial answer is, "I really like the car and clothes," I'm going to ask you to think about this again.

Companies spend millions of dollars in advertising annually to insure that you like their product, so that's the obvious answer.

Let's put the monetary value of your purchases on an imaginary scale next to your income. If the cost of the purchase and maintenance of these material goods outweighs your sources of income – you have allowed your manufactured image to mask your "authentic self." If this is the case, then it is time to check your personal business card.

The You Nobody Knows

I once worked with a young man, Mike, who's job was an entry level administrator. As with many entry-level positions, his salary was low. However, Mike felt compelled to wear designer clothes and drive an expensive car because he believed that his peers earned higher incomes and were economically better off than him. This belief pressured Mike to create a persona that would visually represent financial parity with his peers.

Mike used weekly visits to a hair salon for tinting, styling and facials to support a well-pampered appearance. All of his designer suits were carefully selected and coordinated with designer ties. He once agonized over a purchase of Armani glasses because he thought that the insignia was too small to be recognized without difficulty. This public image provided Mike comfort during the Friday night happy hours when he met with friends.

Ironically, Mike lived from paycheck to paycheck and frequently supplemented his cash short-falls with cash advances from his credit card.

Mike created a lot of self-imposed stress in order to show that he was on the same socioeconomic level as his peers. In his mind, in order to feel on par, or at times, even superior, Mike needed to be draped in designer garments. Looking "the part" compensated for the lack of income. The clothes gave him an edge. Even when Mike had nothing but dust balls in his pocket, he would comment on the quality of someone else's clothes or shoes. In his mind, the clothes converted him from "entry-level account administrator" to "worldly man about town."

The designer clothes provided him with a cloak of superiority. Mike needed this security blanket because he felt socially inferior due to his negative perception of his financial state in comparison to his friends.

Mike's situation is interesting and riddled with irony. At no point during the time that I worked with Mike did he ever reveal that he had any tangible evidence, such as a W-2, which would confirm his belief that his friends were earning more money than he. Mike formed his perceptions based on visual observations. This perception created the nagging sensation that his life was lacking in some capacity, which drove him to create a façade of financial well-being.

The upkeep of the image produced additional financial stress as Mike began to struggle to pay for the car, his apartment and the mounting credit card bills. Eventually, Mike lost his apartment and moved back home with his mother in order to financially recuperate.

Mike's friends and family never demanded that he generate a certain income. His feelings of inadequacy were based on his perceptions alone. Mike determined that he was deficient. His actions were fueled by negative self talk, not input that he received from others.

Now, before you dismiss Mike as foolish, extreme, and insecure, think of some of your own behavior regarding your personal packaging and imagery. While your motives may not involve trying to keep up with the "Jones", the basis for your impeccable packaging or whatever material accoutrement that is part of your personal portfolio is not always because you like to look a particular way for your own enjoyment. You want some form of attention.

Imagine purchasing an expensive designer handbag that has the designer's name blatantly plastered on the surface as if it were a billboard. You did not buy that Prada handbag because you really liked the way it looked. It has Prada written all over it. Unless your name is Prada, what is so attractive about the bag? It's not even leather. You bought the Prada handbag because it has a designer name on it and it is a status symbol. Surely, a no-name leather bag would be just as functional and cost a fraction of what was paid for the Prada handbag.

Attention Grabbers

No one is exempt from this behavior. Let's revisit my shoe fetish. Although, I initially purchased shoes to match my outfits, something happened around the purchase of the 30th pair (maybe it happened before then). With so many pairs of shoes in my wardrobe, I could easily match the faintest color nuance in a blouse or any article of clothing, while most people that I worked with had the standard black, brown or navy shoes.

I took shoe buying to another level by classifying my purchases. Shoes bought without an outfit in mind were "investment shoes." New rules were created: when you see a nice pair of black shoes, buy them, you can always use black shoes. I was spiraling out of control and quickly running out of closet space. I became caught up in the "shoe diva" persona that began as an innocent interest in shoes.

The extensive collection of shoes generated a lot of attention for me. While I liked the shoes, I discovered that I liked the attention much more. I began to think of myself as a shoe savant, an authority regarding the craftsmanship, comfort and color of shoes. The compliments that I received each day stroked my ego and made me feel good. My coworkers started to refer to me as a "shoe diva." I was frequently consulted regarding where to purchase shoes or which styles would be appropriate for a particular outfit.

This new social responsibility added to my addiction to purchase shoes, but it also made me feel good. Although I wasn't going broke in the process, I was definitely TYAR, showing total disregard for delayed gratification.

Why Do We Do It?

The human mind is so complex. From what I have observed, people all want the same thing: to be accepted, loved, appreciated and valued. You and I want to feel special.

The sensation of "specialness" manifests itself differently for each person. No one is immune. Not you, you say? Okay, but think about the activities in which you engage or the sororities or fraternities or church activities in which you participate. Just think about it. Unless you are home alone, simply reading this book and other paperbacks all the time, you want to be involved with other people and you want them to like, admire and respect you.

Think about organizations such as "Big Brothers and Big Sisters" that rely on people who are willing to share their time as mentors and role models to children. In addition to being altruistic and kind, these volunteers believe that they are exemplary people, worthy of being replicated in some manner. Anyone who serves as a "role model" hopes to be a template from which someone can fashion their lives. Certainly anyone who volunteers for such a cause must believe that they have something of value that is worth having others emulate.

It is easy to discern that serving as a volunteer to help others is very constructive and contributes to the good of society. However the same motivating factors which drive a person to volunteer for the good of others also serve to motivate a person to create a façade of wealth and well-being: the desired to be liked, admired and respected. The problems arise when a person loses sight of their intrinsic value as a person due to external stimuli.

Media Helps Define You

The marketing that surrounds us sets the tone for creating the desire for designer clothes and brand names which are easily translated into status symbols. Newspaper, magazine and television advertisements send the message that in order to have "value" or be "valued" you must carry a certain credit card, drive a particular car and dress in designer or at the very least, finely made clothes. We are inundated with these daily messages. They often impact the purchases that are made for the sake of public presentation or social acceptance.

At the very minimum, societal norms dictate that you meet the standards for hygiene and decency, therefore, your packaging is based on your definition of how you want to run your "show." When you leave your house, especially for a social function or work, you have the option of going for the simple "neat and clean" look or you can look "fantastic."

Depending on your preference, you may find yourself spending money for outfits and transportation which exceeds your earned income.

If you can not afford the lifestyle that you are creating, you are manufacturing stress that is wearing away your emotional and physical health. This is a large price to pay for the semblance of having it all together.

Enough is Enough

Fortunately, not everyone falls prey to this type of commercial hype or self-imposed pressure. If you are not addicted to name brands - Kudos! However, before you start patting yourself on the back, think about some of the other material trappings to which you have fallen prey. Remember, this does not suggest that you are feeble-minded if you feel strongly about wearing and driving the finest consumer goods that money can buy.

You are interested in making a statement. You enjoy the attention. You are marketing yourself to the world and you don't want your slogan to read, "Hey, I'm marginal and I've used deodorant today." You want your marketing campaign to boldly state, "Here I am world. I am fabulous, well put together and ready for anything!" This gives you confidence and the assurance that you seek as you interact with others in various situations.

Clothes Don't Make the Person

Revisiting Mike's situation: Have you ever experienced similar feelings of needing to measure up to others? Do you think that everyone else is doing better than you? If so, stop. It's not your job to measure up to anyone else. Your life is the exclusive opportunity to set the standards for your self appraisal. Since you manufacture the scale, make the assumption that you are on par with your peers instead of assuming that you are lagging behind.

In the absence of a thorough pay stub review and financial audit, you can never know someone's financial situation. Don't concern yourself with this type of mental machination. Your evaluative lens should always be pointed inward for self review.

The thoughts and words that you speak internally must always be kind. Let's set the record straight – you are fabulous. You were fabulous when you crawled out of bed this morning, in your crumpled pajamas.

The things that make you fabulous are not on your backside, are not parked outside along the street and are not because of the job title that you hold. You are fabulous because of your intelligence, character, and spirituality. You are fabulous because of your charisma, energy and drive. You are fabulous because of your generosity, compassion and humanity. It is not the external packaging that determines the essence of your being. It's what's going on in your mind that counts.

You must program your mind to reinforce that these attributes are a part of your being. Next, you must ensure that you are complying with the list of superlatives that you have selected to define yourself. Soon you will find that you have become an attention grabbing, attractive person who exudes a magnetic personality.

If you possessed all of these characteristics, people would be drawn to you naturally. You would not have to worry about designer clothes or a fancy car. These attributes are appealing. People want to be surrounded by folks that possess these characteristics; they work like pheromones.

But, I Like Shoes

If you have searched your soul and determined your motivation for making purchases is not due to any feeling of inadequacy or lack of confidence but simply "you've got to have it", that's okay. I can relate.

I'm not going to give up shoes, but I refuse to let my love of shoes drive me into the poor house. Anyone who *really* knows me knows that I am extremely thrifty. Correction, I'm down right cheap. I have never paid full price for anything – especially shoes. Knowing this, I shop very carefully for my shoe purchases.

If you must have certain material goods, then purchase them on sale or look for bargains. You've got to be sensible about how you spend your money. Nothing, I repeat **nothing**, is worth creating a financial nightmare. If you must have your indulgences, and I completely understand, be a prudent, informed consumer. Don't believe the hype of advertisement and always comparison shop. Here are some shopping tips to keep you looking as if you're "living large" when you're actually living moderately and on a budget:

1. **Buy clothes out of season:** If you absolutely must wear designer clothes, then make your purchases out of season. Purchase winter clothes at the beginning of spring and summer clothes in the fall. Merchandisers are anxious to clear their racks to make room for seasonal fashions therefore these clothes are drastically marked down.

2. **Buy on sale:** Make a vow to never pay full price and stick to it. Look for sales. Always comparison shop before making your purchases. Take a note book with you in order to carefully write down the location of the store where you spotted the lowest price. Always keep your receipts in case the item goes on sale within 30 days of your purchase. You will be able to take it back to the store and get the sale price. This usually works for most purchases – except cars.

3. **Shop at discount stores:** Not every article of clothing has to be made by a designer. Purchase clothes that fit well and look good on your body

type. Don't be overly concerned about who made the clothes. There are plenty of "no name" styles available that look just as nice. Some designers have less expensive labels at discount stores like Kohl's and Target. Check out discount stores for stylish accent pieces and casual shoes. Avoid trendy clothes and synthetic fabrics. Trends are fleeting and synthetic fabrics do not wear well.

4. **Buy good quality foundation pieces:** Foundation pieces are those timeless clothing staples that everyone who enjoys clothes has in their closet: the navy blue suit, black and beige slacks (Definitely a black dress if you're a woman). Invest in good quality "all weather" wool for these pieces. Women, accent your garb with costume and silver jewelry (less costly than gold) and scarves. Men, use ties with interesting designs and patterns and a stylish, yet inexpensive wrist watch to highlight your clothes. Use the accent pieces to change the mood of your clothing. Select basic styles that can transition from work to play seamlessly.

5. **Visit thrift and consignment stores:** Don't say yuck. Check out the stores in the high rent districts. You'd be surprised at the quality and variety of clothes that are available. If you are addicted to designers, then you can hit the jack pot and load up on suits, coats (even fur coats) and jewelry for a fraction of the original cost. The clothes are always laundered and well maintained in order to receive space in the store, so you don't have to worry about buying something that has not been properly cleaned. (Note: I wouldn't buy shoes from a thrift store, but that's my personal preference.)

6. **Use coupons:** In the Sunday paper, the major department stores generally run their featured weekly ads and include a coupon that when presented translates into extra savings. Cut the coupon and scour the ads for clothes, house wares or whatever you need. Keep the coupons in your wallet or car's glove compartment so that you can always have them with you when you leave the house. You don't want to run the risk of buying at full price.

Shopping can be therapeutic; it makes you feel good about your appearance and boosts your confidence. However, this should not be your main source for feeling good about you. In addition to creating a well polished exterior, spend twice as much time developing your character and intellect. This is especially helpful if you are feeling that you aren't measuring up to others. Make a commitment to implement personal changes that enhance your life and add to your character.

Be All You Can Be

If you think that the "fabulous" list previously mentioned is out of your reach, reconsider. Carve out some time that you would normally spend in the malls, boutiques or watching television and spend time investing in yourself. Expand your mental capabilities. Broaden your knowledge of general subject matter. Improve the quality of your conversation.

People are drawn to well-informed, intellectual and interesting people. Cultivate yourself so that you feel comfortable joining conversations in social gatherings which include a wide range of topics spanning from current events to pop culture. Commitment to lifetime learning and expansion of your mental capability is the best form of self-marketing available. The more you know, the more interesting you become. Try some of the following activities to get started:

1. **Be familiar with current events:** Read the paper or watch the news each day. Stay informed regarding what is going on in the world. You are a taxpayer (if you used all the steps outlined in Chapter 3, then you should be employed now.), understand the political and legislative environment in which you live. This provides you with data to generate informed opinions and thoughts; two ingredients for a stimulating conversation.

2. **Read something from the best sellers list:** This is a great way to start a conversation. You don't like to read? No problem. Go to Amazon.com and read the book summary and a few reviews. Now you have enough information to form an opinion and join in a conversation or start a conversation. Better yet go to a book signing and hear about the book from the author's mouth.

3. **Watch an evening magazine show:** You want to stay versatile. Not every situation will demand the mental gymnastics of discussing world events and politics, so you need a repertoire of light and airy subjects. Avoid the temptation of gravitating to ESPN every time you turn on the television. Occasionally watch a magazine show to hear the Oscar buzz or Hollywood gossip. Sure this is real fluffy, insignificant stuff, but it's also fun and conversational. Gather your material so that you can join in the latest conversation about Michael Jackson. This is easy.

4. **Attend cultural events:** Anybody can go to the movies or rent a video tape or DVD, but how often can you get to see a live performance? Learn to appreciate the arts. Attend an afternoon performance and benefit from the matinee price. Check out local

theater; it's great entertainment and reasonably priced. Venture to New York City. Broadway tickets can be purchased cheaply half an hour before show time.

5. **Care about something other than yourself:** Each day should begin with the simple realization that you have been provided with another opportunity to be alive. Don't crawl out of bed fretting over what you don't have. Instead, jump up focused on the blessings that you have. Get involved in a community or social cause: help with voter registration, help beautify your neighborhood, help somebody learn how to read or become computer literate. Think of something. Become like that person who thinks so highly of him or herself that they want to be a role model. In addition to building your character you'll be surprised how this aids your self-esteem.

6. **Cultivate a hobby:** Nothing remedies the preoccupation with other people's business better than occupying all of your time. Visit a craft store to find an activity that you think may be enjoyable. Don't worry if the first attempt proves unsuccessful. Visit as many times as it takes to find an acceptable avocation. Anything is better than sitting in the house with the chips in one hand and the remote control in the other, thinking about how you are not as good as your friends and associates. Get up and get going.

Need some help beyond the helpful hints mentioned above? Check out the following websites to start your passage to creating your authentic self and finding the freedom and comfort to be who you really are. You might as well look good (just for the heck of it) while you're figuring it all out, so I've included a mega site for discount shopping as well.

Building confidence and self-esteem:
www.self-esteem-and-confidence-improvement.com

Self-esteem thoughts for the week sponsored by the National Association for Self-Esteem:
www.self-esteem-nase.org/news.shtml

Improving public speaking:
www.toastmasters.org

World news:
www.cnn.com
www.msnbc.com

Volunteering your time through mentoring opportunities:

Girls Inc:
www.girlsinc.org

Big Brothers Big Sisters of America
www.bbbsa.org

Non–Profit Agencies Seeking Help:
www.VolunteerWay.org
www.idealist.org

All (I mean everything!) your shopping needs at discount prices:
www.cheap-discount.com/

Designer eyewear:
www.eye-glasses-now.com/

Making an Authentic Quilt

When I started quilting, I tried to save money on fabric purchases by buying a cotton-poly blend. I soon understood why the instructional books warned against using anything other than 100% cotton. The synthetic pieces often frayed before they could be stitched together.

I quickly learned the value of using pure cotton. Synthetic fabric had no staying power; it merely gave the appearance of looking good for a brief period of time.

Analogous to creating a fabric quilt, the lives that we quilt can either be authentic or synthetic. Just as the pure cotton quilt is durable and purposeful, so is our authentic self. Authenticity should be the basic foundation fabric for our life quilt.

The creation of a lifestyle based on a well manufactured façade is like synthetic cloth; it can not be sustained for a protracted period of time without breaking apart.

The authentic lifestyle supports the lives marked by purpose manifested through service to others, character as demonstrated by unshakable self-esteem, kindness shown to others and a sense of relevance that is defined on personal terms not by trends or peer comparison.

A synthetic life is shallow and superficial, marked by self criticism and self-imposed pressure. These lives are filled with anxiety generated from a need to present a façade that has been incorrectly designed to define your worthiness.

Stop and take a minute to assess the content of your fabric. If you are coming apart at the seams due to financial stress resulting from living beyond your means or you feel the need to buy things to support a façade created in the image of the person you think that you ought to be, then now is the time to reconsider your options.

If your life is being quilted with synthetic fabric this does not mean that you have to continue to create an "imitation life" – get real, stop pretending to be the person that you wish you could be and become the person that you want to be.

Abundance by Planning & Saving 5

(Joining the Quilt Blocks)

> *"If you would be wealthy, think of saving as well as getting."*
> Benjamin Franklin

The quilt blocks take form during the assemblage of the pieces. This process is repeated until the body of the quilt is formed. Alternating patterns and colors that once resembled a jumbled mass of cloth can now be recognized as the top portion of the quilt.

A quilt's construction - the cloth, the strength of the seams and the thickness of the filling - determines the effectiveness of the quilt's ability to meet the simple objective of providing its owner comfort, warmth and security from frigid temperatures. A well constructed quilt accomplishes these effects effortlessly.

Plan to Save or Save to Plan

Life is meant to be enjoyed. This is one of the primary motivations for getting out of bed in the morning or evening and going to work. Finances are essential to enjoying the pleasures that you have identified as important in your life.

Unfortunately, having money is only a partial component to enjoying life. Wise money management is fundamental to providing a life without financial stress.

As we've identified in Chapter 4, merely having access to money is insufficient to creating a stress free existence. Various situations can result in stress, worry and financial ruin if they come about due to compulsively spending and living beyond your financial means.

You may be intimately acquainted with some of these financial woes or you may know someone who is slowly sinking into financial wreck and ruin. If you're still spending gratuitously, enjoying the bounty of your purchases and unsure if you're traveling down the road to financial perdition, here's a quick test:

- Do you experience a cash shortfall each month when the bills are due?

- Are you juggling bills in order to pay them all?

- Are your utility bills arriving with a "red" warning message on the envelope?

- Do you disguise your voice when answering the phone? Or do you screen your phone calls?

- Do you have an emergency fund to cover expenses if you become unemployed or experience a financial emergency?

If you answered yes to any of the first four questions and no to the last, then you are in the financial woe category. Even if you don't feel the stress of your financial situation at this moment, over time, you will feel the effects of spending wantonly.

Financial 911

Hold on, all is not lost, we can fix this. There is a way to safeguard your finances to ensure that your monthly income covers your expenditures and allows you enjoy the pleasures in life in a stress free manner. This is your primary financial strategy. This will help you to avoid drastic measures, such as filing for bankruptcy or having the car repossessed, if you continue to over-spend. It all starts with a **B-U-D-G-E-T**.

If you're like most people, the thought of establishing a budget makes you cringe. It takes too much time. It's too restrictive. It involves too much sacrifice. It won't allow you to have the things that you want and enjoy. This is negative self-talk. This should have been banished after reading chapter 1. Let's move on. This is your budget. It will be constructed to reflect your needs and objectives.

By the way, what are your goals? It is easier to establish and stick to a budget when you have a clear idea of what you are working towards. Think about it. Write it down and place it on your bedroom mirror.

Perhaps you hope to own a home in the future or return to school or start a business or travel around the world or fund a child's education. Whatever your goal, writing it down and placing "the goal objective" in a visible location will help you focus on attaining this goal. This will energize you and give you a sense of purpose for executing and retaining your budget.

Irrespective of your income level you can have an "enjoyable" life; complete with the comforts that you deem important. Anything is possible with saving and planning.

Simple Accounting

In spite of the simplicity of budgeting, this remains one of the most over looked processes in personal money management. How do I know? Well, the number of individuals filing for personal bankruptcy has tripled over the past ten years. That's proof enough for me that personal money management can be viewed as a daunting task. If you don't want a bankruptcy filing to become part of your life's quilt, now is the time to include a budget in your list of household chores.

This is important, so you need to get some paper and list your sources of income. This is your salary and any other income that you receive during the month. Since most billings, rent and mortgages occur on a monthly basis, let's use a month as the time frequency to track expenditures.

Create two columns: incoming and outgoing. These columns represent money that you receive and spend during the month. List all expenses that you incur during a month. Be sure to include the little purchases, such as snacks and meals that may have been unaccounted for in the past. This is important for the initial assessment of your spending so don't dismiss any of your cash outflows as insignificant.

It might be helpful to keep receipts for a month prior to this exercise. This will allow you to note visits to the cash machine and track cash outflow for snacks and entertainment. Although minimal in amount, these "line items" can accumulate large totals, so please don't overlook them.

Now that you have a pay stub and your stack of receipts and bills in hand, you can determine your initial financial picture. List your expenses in order of importance; the items that represent essentials, such as lodging, transportation and food, should be at the top of the list.

Divide expenses that you pay annually or biannually, such as car insurance, by 12 or 6, in order to determine the monthly cost. Be specific. Don't make food a line item; make a distinction between groceries (the things that you need to have in the house in case of a snow storm) and dining out. Include a category for saving even if you are not currently saving on regular basis or not at all. Below is a sample of expense itemization:

Incoming (Net Total)	Outgoing	
Salary: $3,000	Rent:	$800
	Utilities:	$250
	Car Lease:	$500
	Car Ins:	$200
	Gas:	$120
	Cable:	$ 72
	Credit cards:	$100
	Groceries:	$ 75
	Lunch:	$150
	Entertainment:	$250
	Clothes:	$400
	Dry Cleaning:	$100
	Toiletries:	$ 60
	Starbuck's	$ 80
	Music Club:	$ 30
	Gym Membership:	$ 75
	Misc. MAC	$100
	Saving:	$ 0
	Total:	**$3,362**

In this sample budget, the expenses are in excess of the incoming money. If your list is telling a similar story, don't fret. This is a good news/ bad news/good news scenario. The good news is that you've identified your cash outflows; the bad news is that you've got to shave some of the expenses down in order to allow for saving and elimination of debt. There's more good news. After you eliminate debt your cash flow will increase. You can save more money to reach your long term financial objectives!

However, your immediate, short-term goal is to end the monthly stress that you experience when the money runs out before the month. So let's use saving as the universal goal and starting point for revamping the list.

Shave Down

Making alterations to the list is going to be based on what is important to you. Last year, I worked with a friend, Jayne, who completed this exercise. Jayne enjoyed entertainment and frequently went out after work and on the weekends to socialize with friends. Being astute, Jayne realized over time that her hefty entertainment expenses left little money to save for emergencies. Jayne's solution to overspending was to eliminate buying groceries in order to continue her entertainment allotment.

This worked for Jayne because as a single woman she spent very little time at home. Cutting back on groceries allowed Jayne to save and keep her entertainment and clothes allotment.

Using this approach, go back to your list and determine what you can live without. What is non-essential? In Jayne's case, she determined that groceries were non-essential since her home was used for changing clothes and sleeping. For Jayne, a few canned goods in the pantry made sense because she doesn't cook and prefers to eat out in a social setting with others.

While reviewing every non-essential line item, honestly assess the value that this expense adds to your life. If you have a gym membership, this would seemingly add value as it can be used to sustain a healthy physique. However, if you never visit the gym and feast on fast food and snacks, then a club membership is unnecessary. Cancel it and go for walks or ride a bike (and lay off the fast food).

Don't make this a painful exercise. Approach this exercise with the attitude that you are going to eliminate at least one non-essential item. Go over the list as many times as it takes to decrease your expense line items by one.

Scale Back

Okay. The next part is going to be painful because you are going to aggressively make reductions in your spending. If you have come this far, then you have eliminated at least one non-essential item from the list. We're making progress. You've already decreased your expense total. Let's keep the momentum going.

You're next objective as you review the list is to reduce expenditures by 40% for non-essential line items thus decreasing the total further. Note: don't decrease a line item where you have listed a minimum balance requirement. This works best on those categories such as clothes and entertainment or any other that has a variable balance.

Here's the challenge, you have determined that every item remaining on the list is essential (even those that may appear to be non-essential); you can not live without this stuff. The items that are staring back at you are as necessary to you as the sun is to flowers. If this is the case, then just as some flowers can live with partial sunlight, then you can live with partial spending on your remaining line items. Let's get to trimming!

I'm not a coffee drinker. However, I understand from those who drink coffee that a good cup is vital to starting their day. Perhaps you have a line item devoted to coffee. If you enjoy coffee at Starbucks each morning, you are spending an average of $3.50 per cup each day. I have been told this coffee is so awesome that it is worth every cent it costs. I have no doubt.

Since the coffee is still on the list, this is essential to you. You can have the coffee, but now you've got to spend less on coffee. No more "grandes"; you have to move to the smaller size. Try that for a week, you'll need to test this out because you'll probably go through some type of withdrawal. Try to remember that in the long run you've decreased your caffeine intake and saved some money.

If you survive the smaller coffee size intake, try substituting one or two days with coffee from home or purchase from a convenience store. Perish the thought that you're "slumming"; you're scaling back, there's a distinct difference. You are making a conscious decision to spend less money on a "luxury" item. Starbucks coffee is a "luxury" item because it is a high end coffee brand. There are other less expensive alternatives available.

If you need to reduce your clothes expenditure, then revisit chapter 4. There are plenty suggestions regarding how to shop for bargains that will help reduce your clothing expenses. However, if your closet is bulging with outfits and shoes, challenge yourself with the goal of reducing your spending for this category by 75%. You are probably buying clothes because you enjoy shopping not because you need clothes.

This is tough. You're deciding to spend less money on an activity that you enjoy. It may not feel good. You may feel as though you're making sacrifices. You work hard and you want to enjoy your money. Try not to dwell on the notion that you are making sacrifices; concentrate on the fact that you are delaying gratification.

Delaying gratification means that you will be gratified at a later time. Sacrifice means that you are completely giving up the opportunity for satisfaction. This is not the case. You will be gratified and satisfied when you eliminate debt and establish savings. Remember, that's your ultimate goal. You will add enjoyment to your life when you conclude this process.

When I went through this exercise several years ago, I had to avoid some of my favorite shopping spots in order to stay away from temptation. I kept my goal of home ownership in my mind every time I thought about buying "just one pair" of shoes. Do what you have to do in order to make your personal scale-back objective successful.

During this phase, gradually reduce your spending over a period of months. Select the time frame that you find most comfortable. As you gradually reduce your spending in the "non-essential categories", increase your credit card payments to continue your debt reduction.

Create a process where you have an inverse relationship with spending and debt reduction. Spend less money on non-essentials while increasing credit card payments. Siphon off a few dollars to place in a savings account. However, stay focused on eliminating your credit card debt. The interest that you are paying far exceeds the interest accrued on a savings account.

At the end of six months, review your current financial situation with your initial assessment. Look at the advances that you've made. You've made progress. You're saving money. You're moving closer to your goal.

Switch Off

Wow! To reach this point, you made a lot of behavioral changes – don't you feel good? The things that you thought you couldn't live without, you are living with a lot less. It doesn't seem that you can do anymore to work towards your goal. But that's where you're wrong. Let's step out a little farther and take this budget to the max. It's time to switch off some of the remaining spending in the non-essential categories to your savings line. I know you have "siphoned off" a few dollars over the past few months and you may have accumulated a small balance. If you accomplished this goal, fine. You should be proud.

Once again, review the outgoing expenses of non-essential items. Look for opportunities to make additional reductions that can be placed directly to saving. This is going to involve some creative thinking since you've been budgeting for a while and made adjustments regarding spending and behavior. This stage is what I call "budget boot camp" as it challenges you to consider further reductions with the remaining categories.

I didn't say that this was easy. I mentioned that it was worthwhile and in the long-run you would feel better. Steady yourself and look at your grocery line item. Can you switch off $10 in this line item to move to savings? If you use coupons and purchase store brand for some items, maybe you can do it. Consider switching off dollar amounts from categories such as entertainment, clothing, travel and music. Any variable expense will work. Use multiple categories to spread the reduction around and lessen the discomfort of making additional reductions. Place the money in your growing savings account.

Don't Forget the Fun

Now that you've scaled back your spending, finding less expensive entertainment alternatives is vital to helping sustain the changes that you've made. You don't want to sit around your home looking at television, reminiscing about the good old days when the Cosmopolitans flowed freely and a restaurant menu was a fashion accessory. Check out the internet for free stuff! There are plenty of sites that offer free perfume, sunglasses, games, etc. Get on the computer and surf around. If you don't have a computer, go to the free library. Most free libraries have computer banks that can be used free of charge. You'll be surprised at what you'll find. Be careful to avoid the freebies that are offered as an introduction to more costly services.

Don't forget to check the entertainment section of your local paper for free concerts. Some of the museum exhibits have free admission during certain times. If you're lucky, you might find a free reception to grab a glass of white and some light refreshments.

Who says that fine dining has to be a distant memory during your budget renovation? Visit a restaurant school; you'll eat good food prepared by budding chefs at a reasonable price. Better yet, check out your local high school for adult evening classes that offer various cooking courses. These sessions usually cost about $25 - $55 and you get to eat and socialize during the class.

Avoid Temptation

Let's revisit saving. Establishing a statement savings account is a good place to start in order to develop the habit of putting money away. This is especially convenient if you have a lot of debt to erase and can save a small amount like $5 or $10 dollars a month, while going through the debt eradication process. Additionally, if you are not accustomed to saving, perhaps you have not developed your financial knowledge of the various savings and investment vehicles available. That's okay. This will come in time. Your thousand mile financial journey began with your first step – realizing that you needed to make changes in your money management style.

When you accumulate $500 in the savings account, move the balance into a certificate of deposit (CD). The interest rate is a little higher than the savings account and you will not be able to access the money for an established time period (without withdrawal penalties).

It is important to make this money as inaccessible as possible. You have delayed gratification for a few months. Seeing $500 dollars in a savings account may prove tempting for a brief vacation get away or a shopping spree. Don't test yourself during this time period.

Continue your budget strategy. As you accumulate $500 balances, continue to purchase CDs. Ladder the maturity dates, however, don't extend the time period beyond your expected timeline for the planned use of this money.

I suggest using savings accounts and CDs, assuming that you are saving for some goal with a timeline of 2 – 3 years and you're a novice regarding saving and investing. However, if you are more sophisticated and have larger amounts to save, place your money in a money market fund. Money market funds yield higher returns than savings accounts and CDs.

Be advised that money market funds have a minimum balance that must be maintained in addition to a minimum opening balance. Shop around to locate funds that will waive the opening balance minimums if you use an automatic investment plan. This is a service that automatically deducts a specified amount from your bank account each month and deposits it into the money market fund.

Now you're on the right track. You've changed your relationship with spending and cultivated an interest in saving. Take time to learn more about money management.

Get Saving Savvy

Regardless of your starting point in this journey, after a year you should be in a position which shows you have gained better control of your finances. Don't you feel great? Sure you may have farther to go in order to attain your goal, but you've made a conscious decision to stop living recklessly for the moment and plan constructively for your future. This is quite an achievement.

Continue to strengthen your resolve to live debt free and plan properly. Here are some suggestions to help your quest to sustain financial control:

1. **Become financially fearless**: Visit your local library and borrow books about money management basics. Read periodicals that focus on investing. Learn to distinguish between saving and investing. Saving is the accumulation of funds for use in the short-run (three to five year time period). The emphasis is placed on saving instruments that provide easy access and emphasize income preservation. Investing involves a longer time horizon (greater than five years) and may be placed in instruments that focus on capital accumulation. Take time to learn the terminology and types of investments available.

2. **Put yourself on the payroll**: As you create your budget, be sure to include an expense line that covers a weekly allowance. This allowance should cover lunch, toiletries and a small entertainment allotment to last until the end of the week. Place any residual change in a basket at the end of the week before placing the next week's allowance in your wallet. At the end of the month, gather the loose change and put the balance in the savings account. Conversely, if you spend your allowance before the week is concluded,

you must learn to walk around with dust balls in your pocket.

3. **Practice the art of Zen**: You don't have to be a Buddhist to study self-discipline. During your period of behavior modification and intense delayed gratification, practice self-discipline attained through meditation and concentration of determined goals. This is a solitary process. Avoid people who can not support you and your effort to make the necessary life changes.

4. **Cover the basics:** If you are eligible to participate in an employer's plan such as a 401(k) or 403(b) plan, enroll as soon as you are able. These plans deduct contributions from your gross income amount, so you are unaware of the money coming out of your pay check. This allows you to put long term retirement planning on auto-pilot while reestablishing your short-term financial situation.

5. **Plan your purchases:** Eliminate impulse buying by writing down your plans to purchase. Use this process for everything that you buy from groceries to frying pans. Don't leave home without a list of your intended purchases. Avoid taking friends along to make shopping a social event. If you're a "shopaholic" make your trips to malls and stores quick and uneventful. As you gain better control of your finances and impulses, you can take more leisurely shopping trips – but never leave home without your list.

6. **Cut up your credit cards:** If wanton use of credit has been a problem, cut up the cards or at least take them out of your wallet. Learn to use cash only. You can not successfully pay down debt while continuing to accumulate more debt. If you have multiple cards,

after you clear off a balance destroy the card. Limit the number of credit cards that you possess to no more than two major credit cards. Forget the retail credit cards. Stick with the major credit cards that offer some type of reward program. Although you are going to use the card conservatively (never charging more than you can pay in full when the bill is received), you might as well earn credit towards hotel stays, air travel or whatever benefit that is attached to the card.

7. **Use the Dollar Store:** Check out your area's dollar store for great buys on anything ranging from toiletries to foodstuffs. Make purchases that will help reduce your grocery bill. Substitute dollar store cleaning products in place of expensive brands found in the market. Save big by procuring greeting cards, gift bags and wrapping paper here in lieu of shopping at the card store. Aspirin and ibuprofen are also available at these stores. Need a gift? Pull together a theme gift basket using goodies obtained from the dollar store. Everything from baskets to shrink wrap can be found in the dollar store. Look around and load up on the savings.

8. **Party over here:** If you like to be surrounded by friends, food and frivolity, then entertain at home. Prepare a few light snacks and non-alcoholic punch. Invite your friends and ask them to bring a bottle of their favorite beverage. You only need to add soda and juice for mixers, music for dancing and board games and playing cards for socializing. Make the evening so much fun that someone else will want to host the next get together.

9. **Rent movies from your local library:** Slash your entertainment budget further by renting videos and DVDs from the nearest branch, if they offer this

service. A participating branch will rent the latest movies as well as the classics for about one or two dollars for a three day release. The rules vary among the different branches, but the savings make it worth checking out. Make some popcorn (from the dollar store) and watch your movie in the comfort of your home.

Think creatively and optimistically. Don't view the changes that you're considering as a decrease in the quality of your life. You are increasing the quality of your life. As you free up finances you will sleep better and feel more in control of your life. Soon you will notice that you're moving closer to the vision that you have for your life.

Need more motivation and information about debt elimination, saving and investing? Check out these websites:

Saving, Planning, and Budgets (I love this site):
www.personal-budget-planning-saving-money.com

Debt Counseling:
www.ameridebt.org

The Investor's Clearinghouse (Retirement Planning, Investment Fundamentals):
www.investoreducation.org

Financial Calculators:
www.tcalc.com/calculators.htm

College Planning:
www.savingforcollege.com

Mutual Fund Education Alliance:
www.mfea.com

Free Stuff:
www.totallyfreestuff.com
www.thefreesite.com/

Joining the Quilt Block

The design of your life quilt is determined by the pieces that form the panels. Your life quilt is meant to provide a warm, secure and a comfortable lifestyle. This is a reasonable expectation that can be achieved as long as saving and planning are blocks contained within your life quilt's composition. These are two essential "blocks" that must be joined together in order to have the abundant life that you desire and deserve.

To have an abundant lifestyle means that you possess sufficiently ample means to handle your life business. You can have more than enough, with proper planning and saving. Realize that everything you want to have for your life is within reach.

Free yourself from the notion that life was meant to be wrought with financial strife and struggle. True, many things that are worthwhile are challenging in the pursuit of attainment.

You have demonstrated that you are up to the challenge of revamping your relationship with money. By identifying your spending habits and changing behaviors that detract from your ability to save, you move closer to the goal of living comfortably.

Juggling bills and amassing credit card debt prohibits you from affecting a plan for the future as you are constantly facing the immediacy of paying off debt. There can be no security for your future without savings. Savings provide the financial cushion for emergencies as well as the funding for realizing goals and objectives (i.e. home ownership, education, vacation, retirement or a business start-up).

Enjoy life by living in the present, however, stay focused on your long-term plans by 1) creating a life development plan, to be written in pencil (life is not static, so your plan should reflect this fact), 2) create a strategy to implement your plan, 3) devise tactics to bring your strategy to life and 4) periodically review your plan to ensure that you are staying on track. Don't let reckless spending in the short-term derail your future plans.

Commit yourself to completely eradicating behaviors that would return you to a debt and stress filled lifestyle. The "sale items" purchased on credit today, soon revert into costly goods months later as you struggle to pay off balances for things that you had to have at that moment.

Keep in mind you are creating a plan for your life; a beautiful pattern comprised of hopes and dreams. These dreams are attainable, if you take the time to fashion a plan, financially prepare and initiate a process to make things happen.

As stated in the introduction, your goal is to turn life dreams into life schemes. The "schemes" are the patterns that are strategically placed to bring your ideas into fruition and create your life's design.

Minimizing Stress, Maximizing Health 6

(Adding Borders)

"Health is not simply the absence of sickness." – Hanna Green

After the quilt blocks have been attached, the border is added to form the quilt's perimeter. This is the final fabric addition before stitching the top and backing together. Without the border, the quilt design is apparent. However, the addition of the border makes the pattern design stand out boldly due to the effect of its contrasting color.

The border determines the final dimension of the quilt as well as establishes the parameters for the width and length of the filling and backing.

A Healthy Lifestyle

It seems ironic that the main energy source that powers our lives – our health – is often neglected or taken for granted. Although we spend a great deal of time planning for the future, fixating on our physical imagery and acquiring material things, the state of our mental and physical well-being is left to chance. In fact, we further diminish our physical and mental state by involving ourselves in stressful habits that erode our bodies and minds over time.

Lifestyle is a broad topic. For our discussion, I have chosen to limit the topic to the areas in our lives that create stress regarding employment, relationships, money management and body image.

There are many topics regarding lifestyle management that are important and applicable to creating a healthy lifestyle. As I indicated in the introduction, I am not attempting to address lifestyle matters that can be perceived as "disorders." This is not the focus of this chapter.

The topics contained in this chapter are intended to provide suggestions and encouragement that can be implemented through self-control and behavior modification.

If you believe that you are contending with an issue that requires the intervention of a trained professional, such as a psychologist, psychiatrist or other medically trained counselor, then I encourage you to do so.

This chapter will examine a few circumstances that generate stress and provide some alternatives for constructively handling these situations. You might be surprised to find that you are subjecting yourself to a stressful lifestyle without being aware of its damaging effects.

Job Stress

In previous chapters we discussed how a less-than-satisfactory job can affect your ability to engage enthusiastically on the job. However, there are other types of job stress caused by starting a new job, assuming additional responsibilities, returning to work after having a baby, or reentering the work force after an extended absence.

Although the circumstances are different, the physical response may be similar, depending on your capacity to manage the change that is happening in your life. Your ability to handle stress will determine the method used to resolve your work situation and return to mental serenity.

As you experience stress, your body will seek a coping mechanism to help countermand the instinct to stay in bed with the covers over your head. Your inability to get up in the morning does not stem from exhaustion. It is your body shutting down in an effort to replenish it's energy for continued survival.

Continued survival? Absolutely! If you are in a situation were you hate your job or have a new boss, new responsibilities or new baby, you must appear at work and function as if you are not mentally reprogramming yourself to handle a challenging situation. The mental gymnastics of coping can chip away at your mental and physical health.

It starts with fatigue. If you are juggling a new baby and a job, fatigue is common. However, assuming new job responsibilities and feeling ill-prepared to handle the job can be equally exhausting. Your feet feel as though they are encased in cement every morning when you're faced with the realization that you have to go to work. Sleep becomes a hobby; those periods of loss consciousness are a refuge from an existence that you no longer want or feel ill-prepared to face.

As you prolong the agony by failing to identify the root cause of stress, you begin to have headaches. At first, your headaches are like a dull ache at your temples; these are the episodes that you will later remember as the "good days." Over time, these headaches progress to skull pounding, neck aching, temple throbbing events that make you pray for death. Ibuprofen or whatever your pain-killer of choice becomes one of the major food groups as you pop these tablets through out the day, in lieu of a meal.

With all the pain and sleep, you develop hermit like tendencies; going to work and returning home to suffer in solitude. If you have a family, your mood is so foul that housemates secretly wish that you were a hermit so that they could avoid being subjected to your mood swings and temper induced outbreaks. You lash out at your loved ones frequently due to their easy access, using them as an outlet for the anger and frustration that you feel.

If you live alone, you will eventually venture out to torment friends and family as the solitary act of self – deprecation seems insufficient for the level of mental anguish that you feel.

When you emerge from your cave, you look like hell. You may have suffered a skin breakout, have bitten your nails and pulled a few hair follicles out your head as a way of attempting to deal with the angst.

I'm not going to belabor this one. If this scenario sounds familiar, please go back to Chapter 1 and review the tools and suggestions for finding and creating opportunities for a new job.

It is not fun to be consumed by agony and despair, but the good news is that you have 100% control over making changes that can significantly improve your emotional condition.

If you are filled with anxiety and self doubt about your ability to handle the new responsibilities of a promotion or job change, develop a resource network. Find out who has a similar job or has been in the department or company for a period of time. Build rapport and seek advice that can add to your effectiveness.

Consider enrolling in a class or joining an association to commune with other "like minds." Use these interactions to build a network of resources that you can call upon as you grow into the assignment. Periodically remind yourself of your ability. You obtained the job based on your skills and qualifications. You have the capability to perform the job. Build your confidence so that your ability stands out.

If you are returning to work after several years of not working outside of the home, you may feel as though your skills are "outdated". Revive your skills at the local community college's continuing education or lifetime learning centers. In this setting, you can meet other people who share similar situations and experiences.

Don't underestimate the effects of job stress. You might not be aware, so I'm going to tell you what your friends and family want to tell you but are too afraid at this point. Your mood swings are intolerable. You are no longer fun and they want to run when they see you coming, but they cringe imagining the consequences of fleeing and being caught.

These people love you, but they are going to grow tired of your foul mood and erratic behavior over time. They want to see you happy. Make the changes today and stop accepting the headaches and mood swings as a normal part of your life. These seemingly insignificant maladies can progress into more serious physical ailments if left unattended.

Try some of these tactics to alleviate your anxiety:

1. **Enroll in a Continuing Education class**: Community colleges generally have curriculum devoted to lifetime learning, business or career skills. If you're feeling a little uncertain about your ability to handle your new job responsibilities, enroll in some of the courses. Classes are non-credit course work focused on business writing, customer service techniques, leadership, presentation and supervisory skills. Course availability and topics vary upon location and interest. This is also a great place to network and create your own support group.

2. **Chat it up online:** New parents battling fatigue and guilt and folks returning to the work force, can find several support organizations and chat groups on the internet. Search the web and find a group that meets your needs. You will soon find that you are not alone; there are others who share a similar experience. You may also get some great advice and helpful hints from other new moms who are juggling parenthood and work or learn about professional counseling and networking opportunities available to work re-entrants.

3. **Leave work at work:** Make it a habit to leave work issues at work. Don't regurgitate work war stories at home. Use your home as a vessel to relax and

unwind. If someone at work annoyed or angered you, leave those feelings at the office. Concentrate on regaining calm and perspective with your family and friends.

4. **Build your self-confidence:** Some of the uncertainty that you feel may be self-imposed. Why do you feel that you can't do the job? Did your supervisor express concerns regarding your work performance? If not, you are creating your own stress with self-doubt. Believe in yourself. You were placed on this earth to do great things. Make a list of all the accomplishments that you have achieved. Review your list before you leave for work each day. Remember the difficulties that you may have overcome in the past. Reflect on the fortitude and tenacity that has brought you this far. Put your shoulders back and hold your head high. Let your mental message reinforce that you are going to perform well on the job.

5. **Get a massage:** Teddy Pendergrass had a song that directed to "turn out the light and get some burning hot oils." Well, we're not trying to hurt ourselves with this one, but having someone rub the tension out of your back and neck might work. Steal some time away and soak in the tub, then have your partner rub you down. Better yet, go to a masseuse and have a professional massage. You'll feel like a new person afterwards.

When Love Hurts

A stressful job situation is easier to remedy than a bad relationship. A bad relationship requires the input of another person. "Bad" is probably not the right word, because these relationships often provide many "good" times and experiences. Why else would we stay in these liaisons? A relationship only turns bad (oh, this sounds like sour milk) when the people involved have different objectives for the direction of relationship.

For example, you meet that person who is your ideal companion in flesh form: intelligent, fun, goal-oriented, attractive and employed. You go out on a few dates, the chemistry is apparent and the pace accelerates. You want to lay claim and take this "gem" off the dating market. You are confident that your intended feels the same way because the vibes have been good and each date and phone call has revealed that you have much in common. How could they not share your interest in having an exclusive relationship? So you put your feelings out there – fully expecting that your "soul mate" will respond in kind.

Hmm, sometimes, in spite of the free flowing good times and mutual interests, the person on the receiving end does not share the same interest in exclusivity. It would be difficult for you to hear something like, "I'm not looking to get tied down." or "I don't want a one-on-one relationship right now." However, you would get over the initial disappointment, if the person clearly spells out how their idea for the relationship differs from yours. Then as a fully consensual adult, you can make an informed decision to continue in the relationship under a new set of terms or terminate the union and move on. This seems like a reasonable and easy solution to present to an adult seeking a "serious" romantic liaison.

For some reason it never works this way. I believe that there is an unwritten rule that prohibits full disclosure of intentions in the dating world.

In the scenario above, person A openly declares their intentions. However, person B will rarely disclose their objective if it vastly differs from the stated objectives of person A, especially if there is the risk of losing the companionship of person A.

Sure there are times when person B responds honestly, but that's only when person B has some one else or a pool of other candidates that can easily replace person A. Hence, the potential loss of companionship is lessened by the existence of an alternative relationship or relationships.

Does this sound complicated? It should. Romantic stress is complicated, confounding and convoluted. Relationships of the heart are such roller coaster rides. When things go well, you experience the highest high. When things go terribly wrong, you cascade into the lowest lows. Similar to a roller coaster, you feel as though you're twirling around in space, complete with the nervous stomach and giddy feeling in anticipation of seeing that special person. And then sometimes you just want to throw up.

Some of these sensations are most prevalent when "love" is new. This is the time when you are most inclined to act purely upon the sense of sight and you're in the process of setting parameters for the relationship.

It was your attraction for this person that got you to the starting gate. You're in an acquaintance phase that involves learning about other aspects of this person's life to determine if you are really compatible.

There are times during this acquaintance phase when you learn that you are not fully compatible but you continue to pursue the relationship, for a variety of reasons: 1) the fear of being alone; 2) the desire for companionship; 3) the sex is satisfying; 4) the need for entertainment or 5) the fact that you like the person for "right now" but not later. In this sense, your companion is serving an immediate purpose but not really fulfilling your needs as you have determined for a long-term partner.

It is normal to have utilitarian relationships: relationships that serve a purpose. These relationships work best when both parties are fully aware of the nature of the relationship and share the same objective. These are mutually consensual and stress-free connections.

However, in a worse case scenario, you're in a utilitarian relationship, in which you're the utensil and you're unaware, uninformed and have a completely different understanding of the nature of the relationship. This is a stressful relationship.

This is the most insidious kind of stress because you

spend an extended amount of time trying to determine why the relationship is not progressing as you anticipated. Your repeated requests for input receive no response or you may receive half-truths or blatant lies which give you further hope that the relationship is right, real and resolvable.

The person providing the nebulous information (read: lying) is not really trying to be cruel; they are motivated by self-interest. It is in their best interest to withhold key information that would provide you with data to make a decision. In fact, they don't perceive that you are being emotionally harmed – after all- you are finding joy in their company. As far as they are concerned, everybody involved is having fun.

In truth, you are being emotionally harmed. You are filled with angst and uncertainty. These feelings impact your interaction with other people as you find yourself distracted, short-tempered, angry or teary. That seems pretty harmful to me.

As you continue further into the abyss of the unfulfilling relationship you may find that your sleeping and eating patterns are altered. Depending on your overall physical state, you could develop an ulcer, hypertension or some other illness.

You may internalize the situation and blame yourself for everything that you perceive is going wrong. The deeper your self-analysis, the more distant your companion grows. They sense your intensity and in turn seek to remove themselves from the relationship, because "you're just not fun anymore."

As the withdrawal continues, you erroneously look for ways to alter yourself as if this would change the nature of the relationship. It becomes a vicious cycle of self-flagellation and blame.

I believe that it is a right of passage for every man and woman to experience the agony of unrequited love before reaching the age of 30. The key is not to let the agony become excruciatingly long and painful. You have to be astute and aware of the signs that clearly reveal that you and your "companion" are objectively misaligned. This is not easy when you are contending with a lot of stimuli that clouds your judgment.

Here are some indicators that may identify when the relationship is inappropriate for your emotional needs and runs the risk of generating stress:

- After clarifying your intentions, your "gem" makes less frequent appearances.

- Your "companion" assures you that the most efficient means of contact is a beeper or cell phone number, since they are rarely at home.

- An aggressive "sister" or "brother" or some other "relative", but never a spouse (wink, wink), shares their home. That explains the angry reaction to your call.

- Broken dates and promises.

- An aversion to making plans.

- Avoidance of public activities such as parties and social functions. A preference for the movies and other dark obscure places.

- Frequently caught telling lies/half-truths and other tales.

- Does not include you in the frequent outings with friends.

- The "booty call" is your only interaction.

- Constantly borrowing money but never repaying the debt.

- Conveniently disappears during the holiday season or birthdays and miraculously appears afterwards, claiming to have been ill.

- Has a spouse that "does not understand them" or claims, "We haven't slept together in years."

- Baby drama – kids by multiple partners (multiple hostile partners)

- Claims to be "trying to get themselves together" by using your car, money, credit and any other resources that they can squeeze out of you.

- Too busy with work or other activities to make an emotional attachment.

If your current relationship has any of the identifiers listed above or you have cried or felt angry about the relationship within the last week and this is your relationship's norm, then the alarm is sounding. There is a mismatch regarding what you want and what you are receiving from your "companion." Take a minute to assess your happiness. Continuous feelings of sadness and anger are indications that you are not in a healthy situation and emotional stress is the result.

It may be hard for you to truly discern at this point that you're on the short end of a utilitarian relationship. You have made so many excuses and justified your "companion's" behavior for so long that you can't decipher reality from fantasy. Every time you justify an act that has resulted in dissatisfaction and disappointment, you have to create a circumstance or condition that would support the alternate reality (read: lie) that has been handed to you by your "companion."

This is fine if you are a fiction writer. However, if you are an adult, seeking a mutually satisfying relationship, then you must find the courage to move on. Initially, it will be painful, especially if you have concerns about being alone or you are ready to enter into what you define as a "serious" relationship. Unfortunately, if you remain in your current relationship, you will cheat yourself of true emotional satisfaction and not progress towards to your goal. Move on – you're worthy of much more. Use the suggestions at the end of this section to help you visualize your true needs.

The above check list refers to situations where there is no evidence of physical abuse, drug abuse, mental instability or admitted spousal connections. If you are in a relationship where your "companion" places you in a high risk of emotional and physical harm by fighting personal demons, such as alcohol or drug abuse or is physically violent, then you must not hesitate to extricate yourself from this type of involvement immediately.

These relationships potentially endanger your health and life. Remember, you are worthy of a companion that respects and cherishes you as a person. Don't settle for less. Try some of these tactics to help you break free, move on and emotionally heal:

1. **Kick 'em to the curb:** Emancipate yourself from that draining relationship. Remember the rule of thumb if you frequently cry or experience anger over the relationship, then it's time to move on. Reconnect with friends that you may have neglected while you were "occupied" with your companion. You'll feel vulnerable, so stay busy and surrounded by friends and family members who love and understand you. Screen your calls to avoid talking to your "ex". It's over – so there is nothing else to talk about!

2. **Enjoy yourself:** Nothing attracts others like a pleasant disposition and confident demeanor. So what if you are alone? Don't dwell on your lack of

romantic companionship – everything has its season. This means that in time you will meet someone that you like who is worthy of your time. Don't mope and appear gloomy. You are not a charity case. You are a wonderful person who happens to be living the single life. So live it! Go solo to fund raisers, cabarets and coffee houses. Do all of the things that you enjoy. Don't let your solo status stop you from living voraciously.

3. **Get a spa treatment:** Nothing picks me up faster than a facial and a pedicure. Go for the works, if you can swing it financially, have a massage, facial, pedicure and manicure. Leave the spa feeling and looking like a million bucks. Is your money tight? No problem. Go to the beauty supply store load up on facial mask, foot soak, bath salts and moisturizing lotion. Put on some relaxing music, light the candles and incense and have a spa day at home.

4. **Go lightly on the "Cosmos":** Fight the urge to drown your romantic sorrows in the bottle. Alcohol is a depressant. If you are feeling sad and regretful, alcohol will only compound your feelings. Sure, you may meet friends for a drink after work, the company may cheer you up, but don't overindulge on the alcohol. You want to boost your spirits not booze up the spirits.

5. **Draw a relationship org chart:** Take some paper and write down the names of partners in your past relationships. Make a list of their positive and negative traits; the issues which served as a relationship "blocker" as well as the physical characteristics of each person. Look for trends and similarities. Are you caught in a loop of dating the same person over and over again? If so, make a

conscious effort to break the routine the next time you get involved.

6. **Keep an open mind:** As you become more active and outgoing, you increase the probability of meeting new people. Don't hastily discount people that don't fit the prototype of your "ideal" companion. Make your objective to meet people, not to hook up and become involved. Mentally, you will alleviate the self imposed pressure of finding someone to begin a relationship.

7. **Love yourself:** Have the highest regard for yourself. When you are confident and oozing with self-respect, the vibes are contagious. Look at yourself in the mirror – you are magnificent. What kind of dummy would mess up the opportunity to be with you? This person was not worthy of your time, energy and emotion. You terminated the relationship at the appropriate time. Note: This process will work only if you are convinced about the wonderful things that you are saying about yourself. So please don't waiver. Now is **not** the time to nit-pick, hyper-scrutinize and engage in a full fledged fault finding mission (say that fast five times.) This is about loving and celebrating you.

Money Troubles

If you read Chapter 5 then you feel comfortable creating a personal budget and financial plan. You still don't have a plan? Ok, go back to Chapter 5 and work it out.

Now, it's one thing to create money stress because you have mismanaged credit use for your own benefit. However, if you are experiencing money stress because you let someone else use your credit or you allow folks to borrow cash and never pay you back – that's ten demerits. I'm not going to berate you because you already feel bad enough.

You have allowed someone else to use your hard earned money and credit, abuse your generosity and now you are left with the clean up. Chalk it up to experience and never let any one else take advantage of you or your money again.

It's probably not wise to make a loan if you can't afford to never receive payment. Nothing stresses a relationship more than loaning and borrowing money between friends. Yes, that means co-signing for cars and other large assets. If someone needs a cosigner, that is an indication that their credit history is not strong and the potential exists that payments could be late or missed. Avoid tension between you and your friends by making it a policy keep money matters separate from the friendship.

Money worries cause physical and mental damage similar to the types of stress that have been identified already; insomnia, change in eating habits, depression and hypertension to name a few.

If your money worries seem insurmountable, seek professional help through debt counseling. These trained professionals can help you sort out your finances and create a budget for a fee based on your ability to pay.

Consider the fee charged by a counselor as an investment and a way to gain financial freedom. It's time to reclaim the joy and pleasure in your life. Review the websites listed in Chapter 5 in addition to developing your own list of favorites to assist you in this goal.

Body Image

Magazines and television bombards us with images regarding how we should look. One Saturday, I actually watched a show called "Hot Bodies of Hollywood" and found myself trying to emulate the eyebrow tweezing technique used by the stars.

I know my physical limitations regarding what is feasible and reasonable for me to attain. However, there are many people, male and female who view these ultra thin buffed and polished bodies as the gold standard for physical beauty.

Much time is spent attempting to imitate and recreate the visions that we see in the magazines. Women agonize over the diameter of their thighs, the size of their breasts and the thickness of their waistlines. Men spend countless hours working on the attainment of the elusive six-pack abdomen. I can't lie, I like a man with a six pack – but I don't see too many men walking around in "my world" that have wash board stomachs.

Thin Is In?

I am a definite advocate of good health and strongly believe that everyone, who is physically able, should include exercise in his or her daily routine. However, when an interest in physical appearance develops into obsessive calorie counting and skipped meals then it is time to reconsider your relationship with food and your body image.

The messages about weight are transmitted early to our children. I recall when my daughter was four years old, she asked me if "she should go for a diet" (her words) because she had a protruding belly–which is quite common for small children. However, the images that she viewed on television told her that her small but round belly was abnormal.

By the time she reached age five, my daughter knew that she wanted to have a "woman's stomach." According to my daughter, a woman's stomach was flat and convex. I had to admit that I too wanted a "woman's stomach", but I had long since given up on that objective, since I never had a "woman's stomach." In fact, I finally convinced my husband that I am more woman (literally) than Janet Jackson, since she only has a "six-pack" while I have "three liter" sized abs. Who said less is better?

While I have grown confident with my physical packaging, willing to accept some imperfection in exchange for good health and reasonable weight maintenance, I know countless women who starve themselves to "look thin." Sadly, they deny themselves food, existing on diet soda and raw vegetables while walking around hungry. Talk about stress!

Perhaps the hyper obsession about weight is based somewhat on vanity, but more often it is the message that we receive that tells us that thin is better. Women are often dissatisfied with their body images and sometimes overemphasize the importance of being thin.

A recent episode of "The Bachelor" illustrated this point when during an interview one of the bachelorettes stated that she felt that all of the "girls were pretty and really thin." The bachelorette then asked the interviewer as if she needed assurance "I do look thin don't I?" I imagine that the woman would have passed out if the interviewer gave her a negative response.

It is important to monitor your weight. Gaining excessive weight can lead to physical ailments and disabilities. However, there has to be a healthy balance between weight maintenance and exercise. Being too thin is not healthy. Being overly conscious about the weight takes time and energy. Redirect your energy toward eating balanced meals and including exercise in your daily routine.

It Starts Early

If you are a parent of a daughter, (I am specifically addressing girls because it is shocking to know that there are girls in the second grade concerned about dieting.) talk to your child about eating healthy, well balanced meals and exercise. Get involved in a physical activity with your child to help her see the ease in which exercise can be included in her normal routine. This can help overturn some of the messages received about extremely thin body images.

Emphasize that her value as a person is not determined by her weight, but based on her character development. We have to work hard to diminish the objectification of women by exposing our girls to other aspects of their personal development.

Shows like "The Bachelor" and "Joe Millionaire" perpetuate the imagery that women are empty headed ornaments. Well, perhaps those show participants are empty-headed ornaments, since they knowingly appear on television and openly share a man with a dozen other women. They further diminish their self-respect by behaving in a catty and desperate fashion. Ok, bad example, let's move on.

If These Hips Could Talk

I recently read an article that revealed that Americans are the fattest people in the world. I believe this is true. Having traveled to Europe, I know that Europeans do not engage in snacking as much as Americans. We have an abundance of food choices and extended hours in which we can obtain these goodies. We take advantage of the easy access.

While intensely monitoring weight gain and starving yourself thin prove to be physically damaging, completely ignoring the scale has equally damning effects. Excessive culinary indulgences and an aversion to physical activity will lead to weight gain. As you age, your metabolism slows, so the same amount of food that you previously consumed goes straight to your waistline and hips in the absence of an exercise program.

Sometimes the stress that we experience from other aspects of our lives can cause us to overeat. Think about all the romantic "break-ups" that you ate your way through. (I remember one break-up that resulted in a 10 pound weight loss. I could have used this guy after I gave birth to my daughter.) Food is comforting. It seems as though the higher the fat content, the more comforting the indulgence.

Unfortunately, we can not always blame the increased numbers on the scale due to stress factors, sometimes we simply overeat. Most of the functions that we attend involve food and alcohol. While scrutinizing every morsel that goes into your mouth is obsessive, completely jamming food down your throat for the sake of eating is just as unhealthy.

I know that gaining weight is easy and losing weight is difficult. I constantly struggle to maintain my weight. Losing weight is a tough process that takes a lot of discipline and self control.

If you've packed on the pounds to the point where you feel that your health is in jeopardy all is not lost. However, it is important to understand when you are facing a potential health risk, as opposed to moving up a size or two in your clothes. Danger signs are:

- Profuse sweating after mild activity.
- Rapid heart beat and frequent shortness of breath
- Chest pain.
- A weight gain, resulting in excess of 3 clothing sizes.
- Your doctor suggests that you drop at least 20 pounds.
- Family history of hypertension and diabetes.

These warnings are an indication that you need to slow up on the caloric intake and begin some type of exercise regimen. Good physical health is an important factor to enjoying your life without the added stress of the developing ailments brought about by excessive weight gain. Take full advantage of the time that you have on earth by enjoying an active and productive life.

I am not suggesting that anyone should lose weight for beauty enhancement. No way. You must be happy and satisfied with your body, large or small; short or tall. This is not about aesthetics; this is about cultivating a healthy lifestyle. Your eating habits should not place you in danger of having a heart attack or some other illness. You should be comfortable and truly happy with your body image. Do what you must to maintain its physical fitness.

Cover Up with Confidence

Whatever your physical shape, do wear the appropriate style of clothing for your body build. Not every style was created for every body type. You don't have to be petite to be neat and attractive in your clothes. Attempting to wear the latest styles that do not compliment your figure is a quick way to become stressed about the way you look.

I have short legs, so I don't wear short dresses or skirts. Additionally, I don't wear form fitting clothes or expose my midriff because I don't have a "woman's stomach." Eliminating these styles from my wardrobe does not mean that I am not fashionable. I select styles and colors that best compliment my complexion, stature and personality.

As you shop, don't think about the latest fashion trend or gravitate towards the stretch pants because that's what everyone else is wearing. Not everyone should wear stretch pants or the lo-rise Jennifer Lopez-baby-got-back jeans. Select what works best for you.

As you pull together your wardrobe, consider your hair color, hair style, height and weight. Find colors that accentuate the features that you really like. If you are full-figured, don't automatically assume that you have to wear black. Nonsense! Select your favorite colors and coordinate pieces. Accent your eyes and hair with accessories such as scarves and earrings.

Visit a cosmetic counter and have some make-up applied. These professionals know how to bring out your best features and which colors compliment you. Afterwards you'll look and feel great. But don't leave the store yet. Ask the make-up artist to show you how to apply the cosmetics so that you can replicate the technique at home. If you like the merchandise, buy it. If it's too expensive, get color samples and go to the discount beauty store and purchase similar products for half the price.

If you are a large size male, get your clothes altered. Large men need tailoring too. Don't walk around with long sleeves (cuffs that extend beyond your wrist) or baggy pants that drag. Shop at stores that specialize in clothes geared towards your body build. Invest in some classic pieces that can be easily mixed and matched, so that you can have choices for work and casual gatherings. Purchase a sports jacket that coordinates with several pairs of slacks. If you have a round stomach, wear your pants above the convex of your stomach, it looks much neater.

Buy two pairs of well-constructed shoes (black and brown) and keep then polished at all times. If you are heavy you can not buy a cheaply constructed shoe. You need a shoe with a good arch and leather sole to support your weight. Wear lightly scented cologne to exude a quietly confident aura.

Don't believe the hype that you have to be thin to be attractive. Your first priority is to develop a healthy lifestyle, then to work with your body build. Don't engage in obsessive, stressful diet routines that attempt to shave off pounds in an unhealthy fashion. Learn to be comfortable in the skin in which you live – it's your main residence.

Some of the suggestions presented at the end of Chapter 4 may be useful, so go back and revisit for a fresh perspective. The following are specific ideas for tactically reducing body image stress:

1. **Get physical:** No matter what your weight, include physical fitness in your daily routine. Go for a walk, ride a bike, roller blade or garden. It doesn't matter as long as you engage in some physical activity at least three times a week.

2. **Cut back on the calories:** Richard Simmons says "never say diet" and I agree. If you want to lose weight start by cutting the portion that you normally eat in half. Diets fail because people feel deprived. With portion control, you are not denying yourself the foods that you enjoy. You consume less of these foods.

3. **Call in the sugar police:** Sugar intake is a major culprit of weight gain. If you have a sweet tooth and find that you are eating goodies every day, set some parameters around your sweet intake. Instead of having a milkshake everyday, pick a specific week that you will have your shake or whatever sweet indulgence you crave. Substitute fresh fruit for some of the cake, pie and ice cream that you enjoy.

4. **Hold the salt:** Many foods have traces of salt or are prepared with salt – so don't add anymore to your meal. Salt causes your body to retain fluid and also contributes to hypertension.

5. **Drink water:** Sometimes we think that we're hungry when in truth our bodies are telling us that we're thirsty. Drink 8 – 10 glasses a day. You'll notice that your complexion will glow as you flush the impurities out of your system.

6. **Become friends with food:** Stop having an adversarial relationship with food. Food is purposeful and nourishes our bodies. Food does not make you overweight. People who consume more calories than they exert become overweight. If you are interested in losing weight, eat smaller portions. If you eat three balanced meals and include an exercise program, you can maintain or attain your desired weight.

7. **Eliminate late night munching:** Our ability to lose weight depends on our ability to burn calories. Calories that are not used are stored as fat. When we eat late at night and then go to sleep, we lose the opportunity to burn up the stored calories. Try not to eat after 7:00PM. If you must eat, try to limit your intake to fruits and vegetables.

8. **Clean out your closet:** Throw out the tight clothes that no longer fit. Live in the present. If you haven't worn the clothes in the past two years – get rid of them! Don't wait until you lose weight to spruce up your wardrobe – clothes can always be altered. Take an interest in making sure that you look neat and well put together. Knowing that you look good boosts your confidence and helps you feel comfortable with your current physical state while you work on employing healthier eating habits.

If you need more motivation and inspiration to reduce the types of stress discussed in this chapter, check out the following websites:

Newsletter for mothers:
www.simplymoms.com

Lactation support:
www.lalecheleague.org

Work force re-entry:
www.40plus.org

Resources for love relationships:
www.trueromantics.com
www.luvshades.com

Relationship advice: all issues covered
www.relationshipdirectory.com

Support for compulsive eating:
www.overeatersanonymous.org

Women's campaign to end body hatred and dieting:
www.overcomingovereating.com

Weight Loss Advice
www.weight-loss-tips-free.com
www.weightloss.about.com
www.100-weight-loss-tips.com

Eating disorders
www.saferchild.org/eating.htm

Adding the Borders

In spite of its significance, the border is not given as much attention as the individual pieces which comprise the blocks and form the design–but the absence of a border affects the entire appearance of the quilt.

In our lives, some aspects of our physical and mental well-being are treated like the quilt border. Situations and circumstances that seem harmless over a period of time can cause physical damage that can profoundly change the design of our life quilt.

Job stress or the protracted effects of a drama-filled love life wear away our resistance to fend off physical maladies over time. Ulcers, hypertension, migraine headaches or nervous tension are some of the possible results of failing to recognize and act upon the signs that are often all too apparent.

An unhealthy relationship with food can exacerbate our physical deterioration. We can readily see the impact of eating too much and exercising too little, while ignoring the damning effects of self imposed starvation. Ultra-thin bodies are hailed as symbols of beauty to the detriment of the self-esteem and self-confidence of both men and women. These behaviors are often overlooked due to the emphasis on reed-like figures as a standard of beauty.

Our bodies and emotions provide adequate signals to alert us when our internal biorhythms are out of sync. Ironically, we often filter out "warnings" and recreate them as acceptable scenarios. This allows us to continue the less than optimal behavior. When compounded, these "scenarios" create self-destructive lifestyles.

Nature has a way of informing us when the paradigm must change. However, it is our responsibility to be self-aware regarding the signals and adjust appropriately. In certain situations, it can make the difference between life or death.

Without a healthy body and stable mental capabilities, it is impossible to enjoy the benefits of a wonderful life. Good mental and physical health enhances our ability to live life fully; it is the border that surrounds and supports all other factors of our lives. Sadly, we never seem to appreciate these "borders" until they malfunction. Let's consciously implement ways to maintain a healthy lifestyle today.

Part 3: Your Life Dreams

Preparing...
Quilting...
Attaching...

Creating Your Vision 7

(Preparing the Top Quilt)

> *"There is nothing like a dream to create the future"*
> Victor Hugo

After the borders have been added to the quilt, the top is placed squarely on the filler (the stuff that makes the quilt fluffy) and muslin backing. It's now time to shape and trim the top so that it fits neatly on top of the filler and backing.

Over the course of piecing the templates and adding the borders the quilt's shape may have loss some of it's symmetry and requires alteration. The objective is to have the top piece aligned geometrically with the bottom half but slightly larger in order to tuck the edges under as the top and bottom are sewn together. It's like creating balance with room to "wiggle."

Connecting the Dots

If you've come this far in your reading I know that the following is possible: 1) you are actively working or at least have a game plan focused toward accomplishing this objective; 2) you are aware of the need to take care of your mental and physical health; 3) you are moving out of your comfort zone and exploring how you can expand your overall ability and 4) you are feeling confident, capable and ready to take on new challenges. This is great!

You need all of these attributes in order to realize your dreams. Dreams and ideas are your vision for your life; it's how you'd like life's design to manifest as you assemble all the pieces.

If you have the desire to radically alter your life design this may appear to be extreme and unreasonable to some people. Sure, there are a few cheerleaders, but the process of pursuing "dreams" may be insubstantial and incomprehensible by those people closest to you who do not understand your life's vision.

Your dreams are transparent when compared to a concrete reality that has consequences. Your associates are quick to remind you to keep your feet planted firmly on the ground and take the safe route. Those closest to you can't or won't understand your need to take a chance or clearly define the vision or passion that is driving you to seek more out of life.

You have come this far and you've taken steps to make changes in your life and you're moving forward. In this chapter we will identify ways to realize your dream vocation through the use of your natural talents.

In order to really pursue your vision, you will have to block out the folks that try to discourage you or make you feel foolish for wanting to pursue your desires. These folks are not trying to be mean spirited. They are not risk takers. Their negative, worrisome behavior and hyper-critical comments are a manifestation of their personal fears. Secretly, these people long to make changes and take chances, but they are bound by their own aversion to risk. Ignore them. You will soon be an inspiration to them.

It is up to you to filter out this noise and understand that these folks don't share your passion. This is a personal pursuit. Just as you did in Chapter 5, when you were establishing your budget, you had to avoid folks that would sabotage your savings plan. Now it's time to limit your discussion about redefining your life's vocation. Your energy is now directed on crystallizing your vision and passion.

Dulled Senses

I've often heard people tell others in need of motivation "find your true passion and go after it." While I believe this is intended to be good advice it is really a silly statement. Your passion is already inside you. You may have supplanted it for several years due to fear, finances and lack of focus, but it is inside you right now waiting to emerge.

If you recall in Chapter 1, you spent some time formally identifying the things that you like to do. Pull out the assessment results and take a look. Were there any surprises regarding the professions that the assessments revealed that were best suited for your interests and skills? - Probably not. There are no real revelations to be garnered here. You know yourself better than anyone on this planet. What has held you back from pursuing your aspirations has been "subconscious numbing." This is the willful numbing of the desire to venture into new challenges.

Unlocking Your Subconscious

As I've previously shared with you, for 20 years I worked in various corporate management capacities during my career. While I enjoyed many of my assignments, worked with wonderful people and gained a lot of experience, I often felt unfulfilled at the end of the year as I reviewed my annual accomplishments.

I could never identify the core of what was creating the subtle void that I was feeling until I read "Waiting to Exhale" by Terry McMillan in 1995. After reading this book, I was angry. I wanted to know how Terry McMillan could write about my life and make lots of money.

I'd always had a desire to write, but I never took the time to set my thoughts down on paper. Then Terry writes a book about the crappy relationships that my girlfriends and I subjected ourselves to in our 20's and she's on the literary road map.

As I read about Terry McMillan's background, I discovered that her initial career was not as a writer; writing was something that she enjoyed. Terry had something to say and she placed it on paper not knowing or caring if she was going to generate money.

Sometimes we complicate the simple processes. "Waiting to Exhale" was Terry McMillan's catharsis to unburden her heart and mind based on her personal experiences. I could have done that as well. I've lived through enough romantic horror stories to create an encyclopedic version of "Waiting to Exhale."

However, I didn't write about my bad relationships. I didn't write about anything. That would have been a constructive outlet to help work through those stressful situations or particularly bad times in my personal life. Unfortunately, I did not have the wherewithal or the foresight or the clarity of mind to see the benefit of engaging in something that I enjoy, writing, as an outlet to help heal the pain of a broken heart or personal disappointment. It passed me by. This is what I call "subconscious numbness."

Subconscious numbness occurs when you supplant your natural gift or talent and fail to use or expand upon it. A person can become numb due to succumbing to distracting externalities (background noise from nay sayers) or stressful situations that lead to withdrawal.

We will always gravitate towards the activities that we enjoy the most. These are the events that use our best skills and natural talents. Oprah Winfrey always liked to talk; most of her activities in her formative years involved being in situations where she could talk or present. So, it is really no surprise that Oprah is a masterful communicator, producer and talk show hostess. Oprah enjoys her vocation. She probably doesn't even feel as though she's working. Oprah is simply living and making a living doing what she loves to do.

Now, realistically, whatever passion you possess may not propel you to Terry or Oprah or any other famous person's status; that's not the point. I used those illustrations to demonstrate that your gifts provide you with a unique opportunity to create energy and usefulness. In the process, you may find personal fulfillment.

I recently spoke with a former classmate at my most recent high school reunion. After several years of bouncing around different industries, Lena began working with a non-profit agency that supports children's education enrichment. During our conversation Lena informed me that she has finally found an enjoyable job working with children.

I recalled Lena at our ten year high school reunion, she was miserable. Lena was in a volatile relationship and hated her job. Lena appeared visibly stressed and disgusted during the entire event. To see her completely contented and personally fulfilled, ten years later, made me happy as well.

Lena finally realized her vision for personal fulfillment and claimed it. In her case it was twofold: emancipation from a long-time drama-filled love relationship and pursuit of a job reflective of her true interests-working with children.

Cause and Effect

Every action has a reaction, which brings us to the second barrier to pursuing vocations that may generate more satisfaction; fear.

Fear is powerful and decreases your effectiveness. Your biggest objection to fully exploring career options that you consider gratifying is the fear that it will generate insufficient money in which to live – nonsense! Your income potential really depends on how much energy you are willing to expend on developing your true interests. Additionally, if pursuit of this dream job is truly satisfying you will find a way to engage in the activity and make sufficient income in order to live abundantly. (You do have your budget strategy now.)

If completely changing careers seems too radical to consider, look for other venues in which you can pursue or gain exposure to your interests.

I recently came across this wonderful website created by a woman who works as an attorney for her "day job" but writes and records "spoken word" poetry as her passion. She has found a way to mesh her passion for poetry with the practicality of a law degree by hosting seminars on publishing law which includes a "spoken word" session.

Piecing together her intellect with her business acumen, this attorney/spoken word artist sells her CDs at the conclusion of these seminars, as a way of showcasing her artistic capability. What a wonderful use of her talents both artistically and intellectually!

Free your mind from the "What are you going to be when you grow up?" programming that was hard coded in your head during elementary school. This is your life. You determine the rules in which you are going to operate. If you enjoy art and have often dreamed about pursuing a career in the arts, make it happen. Don't dwell on the starving artist scenario that is often portrayed. There are many kinds of artsy, creative jobs available that pay quite well (i.e. graphic design, illustration, web graphics, etc.) Do your research and devise options. Research and identify career possibilities.

Don't say, "I'm good at art. I really like it, but I'm not an artist. I'm an office manager." If you're happy being an office manager, fine; you are an office manager who has artistic ability. But, if you're a miserable office manager with artistic ability, look at your skills assessment and create an opportunity to use your skills.

Remember, using your skills does not necessarily mean finding a job in which your innate talent is the main resource for income generation. This is your "innate ability." This talent is intrinsic. The passion is already inside you waiting to be released in the venue that creates an opportunity.

Dreams Deferred

It is equally frustrating when you have had to delay pursuit of your dreams due to life's circumstances.

I have a close friend that has always wanted to become an attorney. As long as I have known Teresa, she has practiced writing her name with "Esq." as her suffix. However, life happened and Teresa married soon after college, had two kids and went through the pain of divorce after several years of marriage. Economic necessity led her to a mind-numbing city job that paid the bills, but did little more. In her heart Teresa longed to become an attorney, nothing else could satisfy her.

After two decades she took the LSAT, applied for and was accepted to Law School. That is passion. It's consistent, persistent and resistant to opposition and obstacles.

Demystifying "Passion"

There is a platitude that says "do what you love and the money will follow." Many people spend a lot of time scratching their heads trying to identify their passion. I once visited an internet chat room where a gentleman was searching to identify his passion. He was so confused in spite of the abundance of advice provided by the generous participants.

Let's save some time. Succinctly stated, your passion is whatever makes you excited. You could talk about this "passion" at length and never tire. Thinking about the activity makes you feel energized. If this is your job, you don't think of it as a job; that's how much gratification you get from this activity.

Does this sound like your current job? Great! Does this sound impossible? It doesn't have to be. Take some time to think about what you've just read and mentally note all the activities that fit the above description, then:

1. **Make a list**: Write down all of the things that you find pleasurable. Compare this list to the functions of your current job and your personal activities. You want to consider all aspects of your life because if you can not create a viable career out of your "joy" then you want to ensure that your hobbies outside of work include these actions.

2. **Evaluate economic potential**: You're not pursing your passion for pure economic gain, but it is nice to earn money by doing something that you truly enjoy. Using the list that identifies all activities that you enjoy, circle the items with income potential. Underline the enjoyable activities that you believe are purely entertaining.

3. **Create contacts**: From the list that identifies potential employment opportunities, indicate folks that you currently know who may be involved in this vocation. Don't know anybody - no problem. Go to the internet and find affinity or professional groups that have some affiliation with your interest. Tap into chat rooms or locate conferences that you can attend to get better acquainted with your interest. Establish a network to serve as resources. (Go back to Chapter 3 to refresh your networking skills.)

4. **Become an apprentice**: Volunteer in order to gain exposure to your interest. Most comics started their careers by functioning in another capacity. They gravitated towards comedy because of their interest and attendance at venues that provided the opportunity to hone their craft. Whatever your interest, frequent those locations that provide the most exposure and occasion for getting involved.

5. **Stop making excuses**: If your dream is to return to school, make it happen. Start with one course. Don't

use your children as an excuse for not furthering your education. Creatively uncover supportive resources that provide child care once or twice a week while you attend classes. Join a study group if you've been out of the classroom for a while and studying feels uncomfortable. Make it a habit to establish a study partner relationship for each class that you attend in order to check notes and get assignments when absent from class.

6. **Stay focused**: My father attended night school for 10 years in order to get his bachelor's degree. No, he wasn't mentally slow, he worked three jobs while attending school. His dream was to have a college degree and nothing could deter him from this objective. Education was his passion. Become so focused on your passion that nothing can take you off track from your destination.

7. **Keep your passion ignited**: Don't give up on your dream. Don't accept a mundane, dull, lackluster existence. Life is an adventure, so keep exploring the possibilities. Tune out the negativity of your spouse, friends, family or anyone that is telling you that what you want is impossible. It's not safe or economically feasible. If you can breathe, then you can achieve. Just go for it!

If you need more stimulation and encouragement, there are many internet sites available to help you pose questions and generate stimulating self reflection. An internet search under "life's passion" will result in over one thousand pages with additional thoughts on identifying your passion and creating your dream job. Here are a few websites to get you started:

Finding you passion and purpose:
www.lifedestiny.com/true/true02.html
www.bwcoaching.com/ezine/idealwork.htm
www.indaspeak.com/passion.htm
www.oprah.com/spiritself/know/pass/ss_know_passion_16.jhtml

Chat Rooms (Business/Finance; Hobbies & Crafts)
www.chat.yahoo.com/

Sites of folks who pursue their passion (while maintaining a day job):
www.claudeparker.com
www.fyos.com

Preparing the Top Quilt

Preparing the top quilt to cover the filling and backing is a time for adjustment and alteration. Your development of clarity regarding your life's vision is your opportunity to make adjustments. No one can tell you what to do with your life. It's all in your head and deep in your heart.

You know how to articulate your dissatisfaction or the void that you feel. However, clarity is missing regarding the next steps that you want to pursue.

There are no magic steps or website references available to walk you through the process. Don't look for affirmation of what you're feeling from family or friends. This is your process. It is personal, solitary and totally self-reflective. Fully engage in the process.

Ask yourself questions to lead you to your "passion." However, I suspect that you already can identify your source for joy. It's the discomfort of trying something new that is stopping you from pursuing this idea, concept or business venture. It is the anticipation of criticism and questions regarding your motives that is holding you back. I understand your feelings. I walked this narrow, jagged road of denunciation and admonition when I left corporate America to start my own consulting business.

Determine your level of risk taking. Identify how you can use your "gifts" to create a livelihood or supplement your livelihood. Don't feel compelled to make a change if you feel that the timing is not right. Remember, the time for change will never feel "right" because it is uncomfortable. Ease into your new pursuit if that will provide you with a more comfortable transition.

However, don't dwell on wishing that you could change your life. Your life is yours to change. Take control of your personal enterprise. As the CEO, make decisions that will yield maximum satisfaction and minimum stress. Confer only with your spiritual being; your board of director. Quietly reflect and meditate to seek assistance with "executive" decisions. This will clear your mind regarding the direction that is right for you. Stay positive and focused on your mission. Everything will work out as it is intended.

Minding Your Own Business   8

(Quilting or Tying the Top)

> *"To accomplish great things, we must dream as well as act"*
> *- Anatole France*

Once the quilt top, filler and bottom have been placed together, it is time to secure all of the pieces. Now is the time to decide whether the body of the quilt should be secured by quilting or tying. (Quilting refers to the stitching that frames the individual templates to accent each panel's design.)

Quilting stitches can be as simple as a straight line or intricate swirls that form elaborate designs. Tying, the quicker option uses strategically placed yarn bows to lock all the layers together. With either option the end result is the same; the top, filler and bottom are locked into place.

Getting Down to Business

So it's finally crystallized in your mind – you want to be your own boss. I've encountered many people who have articulated the same thought; they want to be business owners. If this is your dream, let's figure out how to bring this into fruition. Keep in mind, this is a very long and intense process, so we won't cover everything required in this chapter. However you'll have enough to get started on developing a business plan. This will move you closer to your dream.

Okay, you've been talking about owning a business for years, so tell me about it. Put down the book and describe the line of business that you'd like to venture into. Say it out loud. Thoughts are presented differently when spoken as opposed to being written down on paper. Go to the mirror and tell yourself the business' objective.

Let's keep your outline simple for now, because there is much involved in this process. Our first task is to clearly identify your mission. Your brief monologue should include:

- **Business description:** Identify the product or service that will be the lynch pin of your enterprise.

- **Product origin:** Describe of the source for your goods and services. Is this intellectual property (it's all in your head)? Is this something that you will produce (make yourself)? Will another person produce the good or provide the service (you will be a distributor)?

- **Potential viability:** Detail why you believe there is an active market for your business product. Since this is a mini-brainstorming session – you don't need to produce data to validate your thoughts, but intelligently summarize the reasons why you believe this idea can earn money. As you advance to the point of business plan creation, you need tangible support to identify your market drivers.

- **Funding:** How are you going to finance your biz? Do you need start-up money? Do you have savings to help launch your business? Will you need a bank loan? Do you need investors? Keep it brief for now, remember, you're just formulating thoughts. You're building a mental outline that will serve as a reference later.

Pulse check. How'd you do? Were you able to rattle off without hesitation your business vision? Did you stammer, stutter and stand mute while checking out your nose in the mirror? This can be your secret but if you did the latter, you need more clarity in order to determine what your venture is all about. Perhaps you need to step back and re-examine your motive for wanting to start a business. You need to have a solid idea that you can build upon. Until that happens you need to stay at the starting gate. You don't want your dream to become a nightmare.

People sometimes envision business ownership as a glamorous undertaking. Nothing could be further from the truth. Starting a business is hard work, comprised of long hours and much personal sacrifice. If this is truly in your heart, then you are willing to endure whatever you must do to make your dream of business ownership a reality.

If your business recitation sounded as if you practiced for years, good for you! You're ready to dig in and get busy.

Getting Down the Details

There is a lot of software available to show you how to do a business plan. The prices range between $29.99 and $59.99. I'm sure that they are all good resources. However, since you are starting a business (notice the positive affirmation) and need to use your money sparingly, access the Small Business Administration's business plan tutorial. This is step-by-step instruction that covers everything that you will need to write your business plan. The best part of all is that it is **F-R-E-E**!

Go to *www.sba.gov/starting/indexbusplans.html* and print out a copy of the plan outline. You will use this to walk through the process of putting your ideas on paper.

The SBA's business plan tutorial is very thorough and inclusive. You can complete this information at your own pace. In addition to walking you through the steps, there are several pages available that list resources and address frequently asked questions.

If you use this site and suggestions listed in this chapter, you will be able to craft a salient business plan that can pass the close scrutiny of any financial review.

Who are You?

The first order of business is to clearly identify how your business is to be formed. Are you going to be a sole proprietor, partnership, or limited liability company (LLC)?

Due to the many legalities associated with incorporation, I will not address that formation in this chapter. For your convenience, I included a website reference at the end of the chapter that deals with incorporation. If you are leaning in that direction, seek the assistance of an attorney and a good CPA for formal advice and counsel. It's important to initiate your business correctly to avoid problems later.

Here are brief descriptions of the various business types:

- **Sole proprietorship**: You are the lone ranger. It's the simplest form of business because it is owned by one person – you. However, you need to comply with local registrations, licenses and permits required for your business. Call your local **Chamber of Commerce** to identify the licenses, zoning and permits needed in order to make your business compliant with the law.

    You will let your state know that you are in business by completing a **Registration of New Enterprise form**. It's not that the state wants to wish you well in your endeavor; they want to ensure that they receive the income tax from your business venture. After you are registered, the state will send quarterly invoices requesting submission of state income tax. See, you already have someone in your corner, thinking optimistically about the viability of your business!

You may find this form under the Department of State; The Corporation Bureau.

While you're completing forms with your state, if your business is called something other than your legal name, for example, Michele Claybrook-Lucas Consulting, then you'll need to complete a **Registration of Fictitious Name** to legally identify your business' name (i.e. Career Mosaic Consulting).

Before you decide on a particular name check with the state Corporation Bureau first. The name must be available. There can not be another business operating in your state with the same name.

Have a couple of ideas before you call the Bureau. They will tell you over the phone if the business name is available or not. If available, you'll complete the application for registration of a fictitious name. Attach a check for the fee and in 3 weeks you'll receive a lovely letter congratulating you on the establishment of your business (accolades already!).

As a sole proprietor you will be responsible for paying both income tax and any business debt that is incurred. If your business fails to make a payment to a supplier or you are sued, then your personal assets can be claimed to make payment for business debts.

- **Partnership:** You'll never walk alone. This is a business that is formed by more than one person but is not incorporated or formed as a LLC. Similar to the sole proprietor, partnerships are personally liable for all business debts and financial obligations generated by the business.

If the business can't pay a creditor then the creditor may make claims on the partners' assets to seek resolution.

A partnership is not taxed separately from its owners; it's a "pass-through entity." The partnership itself does not pay any income taxes on profits. Business income "passes through" the business to each partner, who reports his or her share of profit or loss on their individual income tax return. In addition, each partner must make quarterly estimated tax payments to the IRS each year.

Although the income is "passing through", you will have to file a form 1065 annually to let the IRS know each partner's portion of profit or loss.

Forming a partnership does not require any special form or partnership to create this type of venture; simply agreeing to become partners can get you started. However, it is best to stipulate on paper the terms of the partnership, in the form of a partnership agreement, to avoid misunderstandings and clearly identify the rules for operation. The creation and validation of this agreement is monumental and worth seeking the counsel of an attorney.

You will need the same registrations, zoning and permits as the sole proprietor in addition to applying for the fictitious name and registration of new enterprise.

Legally, when one partner leaves the partnership, this marks the dissolution of the partnership. If you choose this option, think proactively and create a buy-sell agreement as you formulate your partnership. This will allow for the remaining partner(s) to buy out interests of the exiting partner, while continuing the business uninterrupted. Again, it is worth the monetary investment to utilize legal resources that will establish the correct language for this type of agreement.

- **Limited Liability Company:** Similar to a sole proprietorship and partnership, profits are taxed once, but personal liability for business debt is limited, like a corporation. Yes, this sounds like a great deal, but not all businesses are suited for this type of formation, so check with the A team (the accountant and attorney) to make sure that this is right for your business.

Are you tired yet from all this pondering about your business classification? Oh it's too soon to grow weary. This is your dream right? Then let's keep pressing on. However, we'll change up the pace before you start writing that business plan. Be prepared to spend a considerable amount of time preparing your business plan. When completed it will be a comprehensive document that outlines every aspect of your business operation.

Research, Resources and Resolution

If there are other folks that have established business ventures similar to what you're pursuing, now is the time to make contact and ask some questions.

You want to know as much as you can about this business. What are the start-up costs? What are the available resources? Are there any particular skills or training requirements? Don't be fooled. All businesses require some investment of training and skills renewal. Even consultants must constantly read, attend conferences and take courses to stay fresh and current regarding trends and issues. Find out what's being done by those people who are already in the business.

If you don't know anyone personally, look in the phone book to identify folks that have similar businesses. Give them a call and ask to meet and discuss their business. Be forthcoming by letting them know that you are interested in starting a similar enterprise.

Come to the meeting with questions and an outline of ideas that you want to "bounce off" of this resource person. Don't come to the meeting without a clue or inkling regarding the direction that you wish to move in. Folks are busy and most don't mind offering some help. However, no one is going to hold your hand and walk you through your process.

If you feel uncomfortable about calling strangers and asking for an appointment – this could be a huge impediment. Being a business owner is not for the shy and faint hearted, especially when you are in the nascent stages of business development. You must proceed boldly!

Read as much as you can about your business. You need to learn everything about the business in order to complete the rest of your business plan template. Be prepared to spend countless nights working to gather and interpret data to make it applicable to your venture.

Don't second guess your intentions, if this is what you want to pursue, bring this to fruition. Work through the SBA business plan template, completing a section at a time. Use contact resources to gather information about markets, suppliers, funding and growth potential. Remember, you are not trying to replicate their business you are creating your own business. What makes your concept fresh, new and different?

Throughout your research stage you must constantly think about your business development angle. This will become your mission statement that will permeate throughout the various stages of your business development.

Give yourself adequate time to complete the business plan. This document will become your "holy grail" as you set about putting your plan into action.

A Business Mindset

Creating a business can be challenging; especially for anyone who has never experienced working for themselves. No one, other than another business owner will ever understand the intensity of effort, drive and fortitude that it takes to get a business up and running from the germination of an idea to developing an enterprise that is capable of creating a steady cash flow.

You must develop a thick skin to protect yourself from disappointment, isolation and at times despair. Your family, spouse (if you have one) and friends can never understand your motivation, drive and intensity. They can not understand how you can work 20 hours a day, make short-term personal sacrifices yet continue to be exhilarated and enthusiastic about an effort that generates little to no income in the first year of operation. They can not understand why you are draining your bank account to put money into something that initially lacks steam. It seems incredulous that you are willing to take on 100% of business risk, in lieu of working a comfortable job with benefits.

It's not their dream. Only you alone can understand that the sweat equity dispensed today will reap benefits tomorrow. Hold on to this belief. You will need this as a reference on one of those days when you hit a low point and you temporarily doubt that what you're embarking upon makes sense.

Miracle Grow

Always remember your two reasons for starting your business: 1) you are passionate about the mission and 2) you want to make money. A business is like a plant, it must be nurtured in order to grow.

You've got to build your business. Network, make cold calls, make cold visits, do direct mailings and advertise. Do whatever you must do in order to get your business in front of your target audience. Find a way to infuse information about your business in every conversation. You are your business and your business is you. You never know when a business opportunity might happen.

Handling Disappointment

Understand that establishing a client base is a long and arduous process. Your first opportunities to obtain business may come from your family, friends and acquaintances of friends; people that know you and wish to be supportive. However, you can not grow your business long-term using the "friends and family" network.

As you broaden your market audience, you will meet new folks, some of them will be cordial, but disinterested; others will be rude and disinterested, but eventually you will encounter someone who is interested in your service or product. This will generate a business opportunity. You must persevere and remain positive. You will hear many "no's" before that one "yes." Some people will waste your time; others won't return your calls. It's not personal. These folks are in their office, worrying about budget cuts, office politics and down-sizing. Their inability to return a call is not about you. Everyone has their own agenda, remember your own. Move on and keep plugging away. Hold on to your belief that your business is valuable and relevant.

Here are some ideas to get you going as you take on the monumental task of business development:

1. **Check with the Chamber:** Most cities have a Chamber of Commerce. This is an excellent resource for business advice, consulting, training and workshops. They generally host monthly networking sessions that provide exposure to other folks in business. This is a great way to make key contacts that may prove helpful to igniting your venture. It costs a few hundred bucks to join the chamber, but it definitely is an investment that is well spent. Join and get involved, don't just carry the card in your wallet.

2. **Attend conferences**: Surf the web to locate conferences for your particular field of business. Identify a travel radius that marks the distance that you are willing to travel in order to attend these sessions. While at the conference, talk to others. Find out about their business tell them about your business. Exchange cards, if it seems reasonable that you may have some connection.

3. **About the business cards...:** I've got to say this because I've attended several networking functions and collected many cards. Vista Print, an online stationary company provides free business cards. I know this because I've received several business cards, from different sources that have "Vista Print printed free at *www.vistaprint.com*" on the back of the card. After reviewing the web site, I learned that for an additional $9.95, Vista Print will graciously remove their advertising from the back of the card. If you're going to use Vista Print, please pay the $9.95 to get the advertising removed. This is your business. The presentation that you make speaks volumes about your business. Letting everyone know that you are too cheap to pay $9.95 to have the advertising removed will reflect badly on you.

4. **Cultivate relationships:** Don't become a collector of business cards. As you attend functions, you'll meet new folks and acquire different cards. After each function, take the time to send a note of acknowledgement, indicating how pleasurable it was to make their acquaintance. Stay in contact by periodically sending a friendly note or calling to check on their business endeavor. You want your network to be vast and diverse. Don't overlook cards obtained from people whom you think are far

removed from your business' objective. They may have a contact that could prove useful in the future.

5. **Brand it:** Brand your business so that it is memorable and distinguishes you from others. Select a logo that you can carry throughout your business card, stationary, brochures and whatever is associated with your business. Back to Vista Print (honestly, I have nothing against Vista Print), they offer limited business card styles. I have several cards for different companies with the same card style. Imagine attending a networking function and trading off cards with identical branding. If you consider your small business as a "mom and pop" operation and you want that perception to permeate to others, then the online freebies are okay. However, if you want to give the impression that you are investing in the overall development of your company, including the small details, then stay away from the freebies that don't offer you the opportunity to distinguish your business. You'll eventually run into other people with your branding. When it happens, you won't like it.

Keep in mind that branding extends to the print font that you use to represent your business. Your font styling is also an identifier for your marketing. Pick a font style that you like and keep it consistent in your marketing materials and business cards.

6. **Seek support:** Whether you are building your business from the ground up or franchising, seek organizations that specifically help navigate through business development issues. Most metropolitan areas have a Small Business Support Center. Regionally, the Midlantic Business Alliance provides consultation and workshops to assist folks just starting out as entrepreneurs. Membership is nominal and it provides access to lots of resources.

7. **Go to school:** Colleges usually have some type of small business development center. These centers are generally supported by the Small Business Administration. They provide offerings regarding consultation, training and workshops and networking opportunities.

8. **Visit the Small Business Administration (SBA) online:** The SBA offers **F-R-E-E** online business training and consulting. This is a very inclusive website. You can find an answer to most of your business questions on this site.

9. **Make it public:** Look for ways to make your business known. Contact your local radio and television stations to see if you can get a spot on the air to discuss your business venture. Send a press release to your local papers to announce your business. Don't discount any opportunity as insignificant. If you're standing in line at a store, initiate a conversation with the person closest to you; talk about your business. It may result in a business lead.

10. **Cold call:** Don't say yuck. You never know what might happen if you try. If you don't want make the calls pay someone else to make calls for you. Do you have limited cash? No problem; offer a 100% commission job with terms that pay a percentage of all contracted business that results from calls.

11. **Keep the financial coffers filled:** If you can start your venture before quitting your job, you won't have a problem with your financial upkeep. However, at some point you'll have to cut the cord and totally immerse yourself into the business. If your funds run low while your building, get a part-time job to keep

some cash in your pocket. However, don't take on part-time employment that will derail your main objective of building your business. Work enough hours to gas up your car and pay for your business phone line, website and other operational expenses.

There are many websites available for advice regarding starting a business. Here are a few guaranteed to get you going:

Key Steps for Starting a Business:
www.bspage.com/start.html
www.bizfilings.com/learning/startabiz.htm
www.startupjournal.com/
www.inc.com/guides/start_biz/

SBA Women's Business Center:
www.onlinewbc.gov/docs/starting/

Is it a Business or a Hobby?
www.irs.gov

Franchising Information:
www.franchising.com/
www.franinfo.com

Quilting or Tying the Top

Similar to locking the top of the quilt to the bottom, as you embrace your entrepreneurial spirit the idea of going out on your own becomes "locked" in your heart. Your initial idea evolved into a business plan. That business plan formed your enterprise's framework. The effort and determination you have expended is evinced by the sweat equity that founded your business. You've taken a chance. The idea of returning to the security of a "nine to five" job is not an alternative.

Your commitment is "tied" to your vision, merging the two together to bring into fruition the dream of success that you believe will happen for you. This is not a hallucination.

Sometimes it may seem incredulous that you have chosen the right course; clients are sparse, money is sparser and criticism is abundant. During these times you are most susceptible to self-doubt which permeates your thoughts like a malignant cancer whose mission is to undermine and derail your objective. Remember that you are where you are for a reason. Continue to position yourself for success.

You are on your way. Seek out other like minded individuals who share your dream of business ownership. Use them as a support system and a network of resources. Know that building a business requires a tremendous amount of fortitude and focus. Understand that it takes five to seven years to build a solid client base. Learn to measure your progress incrementally and celebrate each measurable milestone, no matter how slight.

You have determined that you will live your life without regrets, so continue with your business plan's execution.

Putting it All Together 9

(Attaching the binding)

> *"Go confidently in the direction of your dreams. Live the life you have imagined."* – David Henry Thoreau

After all the stitching and piecing has been completed, the quilt maker will add binding to cover the loose ends to give the quilt a neat, finished look. The binding also helps to stop the ends from fraying and unraveling over time due to age and excess use. In a sense, the binding keeps everything together.

The Finishing Touch

Your moment has arrived; you're at the end of the book. Hopefully, you used some of the suggestions. You're making changes in your life that you once felt too timid to attempt. Or perhaps you're in the contemplative, planning and goal setting stage. It doesn't matter. What is important is that you are going to make some changes that will result in a revitalized, renewed and refreshed individual. One who is confident and comfortable with themselves.

Each day presents an opportunity to make choices about the direction that you wish your life to take. Have you decided that you want your life to be as satisfying and authentic as possible? Have you determined that you are going to live your life without regrets? I have.

A few years ago, I asked myself these same questions. I grew tired of living a "half life"; a life that merely consisted of going to work and coming home. I decided to do two things: 1) pursue some long suppressed dreams and 2) share myself with others. My goal was to merge skills that I had acquired over time with activities that I truly enjoyed.

On a single sheet of paper, I wrote a brief, two paragraph biography that described the person that I wanted to become. At the time, the only part of the description that was one hundred percent accurate was the information that noted my educational background, past work experience and my status as a wife and mother; everything else was based on my dreams and vision for my life. However, I was determined not to be confined by reality but embrace possibility. Below is the first sentence of the bio that I wrote:

Michele Claybrook-Lucas is a business writer, consultant and author of a self-development book.

These words became my objective. I was focused on achieving everything that I wrote on the paper by actively pursuing opportunities and often creating opportunities to bring this vision to life. Was it easy? Not at all. Was it frustrating? Yes, very much so. Was I ever disappointed? Yes, on many, many occasions. Did I ever get discouraged? Yes, however I used the tactics outlined in this book to keep moving forward. Every disappointment allowed me to step back and reevaluate my approach to achieving my goals.

You Can Do This

I am no extraordinary person, so if you want to reorganize your life, this is reasonable and within your reach. We've talked about so much, but I'll briefly highlight some key points to remember as you work on your life quilt's design:

- **Eliminate fear:** Fear is an anchor. It will stop you from trying to step out of your comfort zone and to explore new opportunities that challenge you. Life demands that we approach it boldly. The worst thing that can happen is that you fail. If you make a failed effort, at least you have the satisfaction of having tried.

- **Engage in "honest" self-evaluation:** Make a distinction between what you want to do and what you are capable of doing. Career aspirations that involve skills in which you do not excel require extra work and training. For example, if you like to sing and aspire to become a performer, you have to possess a good singing voice. If you don't sing well (not sure, tape yourself and ask a few people that have no personal attachment to you to evaluate your singing) – take some lessons. Seek opportunities to practice your emerging voice in non-threatening venues but don't quit your day job.

- **Use a gradated approach:** Break your goal into small segments. Whatever your aspiration, there is some venue available that will allow you to volunteer or intern. Non-profit agencies are always looking for folks to volunteer services. If you aspire to become a web designer, offer to design their web sites for free. You can use the experience and exposure to move onto bigger, paying assignments with the references that you acquire from your volunteer services.

- **Be "self" considerate:** Pay attention to your our own needs and feelings. This is not selfish. You need to take extreme care of your emotional and physical well-being. Don't spend a protracted amount of time being unhappy – in any situation – be it a job or a relationship. Be willing to make changes that will enhance and energize your life.

- **Develop professional maturity:** At some point in your life you may find yourself in an employment situation that you hate. Instead of being miserable, program your mind to accept that this is a mere stop in your career life-line. Actively pursue other "well-thought out" options. Staying in a job that makes you sick to your stomach impacts your health and work performance. This can blemish your employment history. However, be fair in your evaluation of why you find the work situation repugnant.

- **Enable others:** In spite of how terrible you may feel at times, there is always someone else who is in a more precarious situation. Extending yourself to help others gives you perspective about your life and serves to improve someone else's life. Commit to making service a part of your life quilt.

- **Make your mental, physical and spiritual well-being a priority:** If you have a wonderful job, great relationship, lots of money and all the material possessions that you desire, it is does not mean a thing if you are stricken with illness and are spiritually void. Be attentive to your body, mind and spirit.

- **If you see a nice pair of black shoes, buy them:** Oh, forget it, that's my rule. Create your own rule of thumb for your life's journey.

Attaching the Binding

Over time, we will all "fray and unravel" due to old age and excess use, if we're lucky. To be well worn and completely used up is the goal that I wish for you at the end of your life.

The "wear" will result from the compilation of the excellent work that you will do (both on the job and in your life while serving others) over the course of your lifetime. The "excess use" will be the outcome of living fearlessly, loving cautiously, embracing change and expanding your mind. I know that these things are within your reach.

This book has covered many topics; each chapter beginning with a quilt-making tactic. If you've learned how to make a quilt while reading this book, great; however, that was not my goal. It would be better for me to show you how to make a quilt, rather than put the instructions in writing. My objective was to show you how to maximize the satisfaction in your livelihood and lifestyle "panels" and provide you with the stimulation to set goals for achieving your life dreams.

The "quilting" of your life happens when you place all three components together.

The three "panels" are inter-related. If you are dissatisfied with your job it will impact your lifestyle. Conversely, an unhealthy lifestyle or lifestyle issues can impact your ability to function on your job, which is how you make your livelihood. Sadly, most of us are too apprehensive to contend with life dreams.

Life dreams are complex and riddled with much uncertainty. You are constantly plagued by the "What if…?" questions: "What if I fail?"; "What if I can't pay my bills?"; "What if people don't like it?"

If you think carefully, you are no stranger to failure. You have failed before – we all have (I failed my driver's exam six times before passing.). A failure occurred each time that you did not meet your planned objective. When that happened, you went to your plan "B" or whatever you call your alternate plan. A devastating failure occurred only if you didn't meet your objective and were permanently incapacitated.

Remember that you possess the resilience to rebound and try alternatives; this is the thread that helps piece your life's sampler quilt together.

I have provided you with the resources to make a start. You must use your energy and optimism to propel yourself forward. Continue to build on the ideas presented in this book. These ideas are sample templates to assist you with your design, but you will create others that will make the quilt personal and very beautiful. Good luck and happy quilting!

Additional resources that might be helpful

"Market Yourself and Your Career"
Jeff Davidson
Adams Media Corporation ($12.95)

– A practical guide to becoming your own career coach.

"Career Tests"
Louis Janda, PhD.
Adams Media Corporation ($12.95)

– More tests (if you're still not convinced) to help you find the type of career that suites your personality and interests.

"Entrepreneur's Ultimate Start-Up Directory"
James Stephenson
Entrepreneur Press ($17.25)

– 1,350 business start-up ideas to help find the business of your dreams

"Simply Essential Personal Budgeting Kit"
Sylvia Lim
Self-Counsel Press, Inc. ($11.95)

– Take control of your finances.

"When Women Stop Hating Their Bodies: Freeing Yourself from Food and Weight Obsession"
Jane Hirschmann and Carol H. Munter
Fawcett Books ($14.95)

– An empowering book that boosts confidence and self-esteem regarding body image.

About the Author

Michele is the president of Career Mosaic Consulting; a career development consulting firm, with an emphasis in work-life balance issues.

She is a graduate of the University of Pennsylvania, receiving a Bachelors of Arts in Economics and a Masters of Science in Organizational Dynamics.

Michele addresses career concerns in her monthly column, "Career Mosaic" featured in "Perspective" Magazine.

She is also the editor-in-chief of "Career Patterns", a quarterly newsletter that offers advice regarding career development issues (**www.career-mosaic-consulting. com**).

Compassionate and committed to serving others, Michele is a mentor at The Center Foundation; an organization that pairs women with other women facing difficult life transitions who seek help rebuilding their lives.

She lives outside of Philadelphia with her husband and daughter.